Discovering
ETHIOPIA

Ethiopian Tourist Trading Enterprise
PO Box 5640, Addis Ababa, Ethiopia

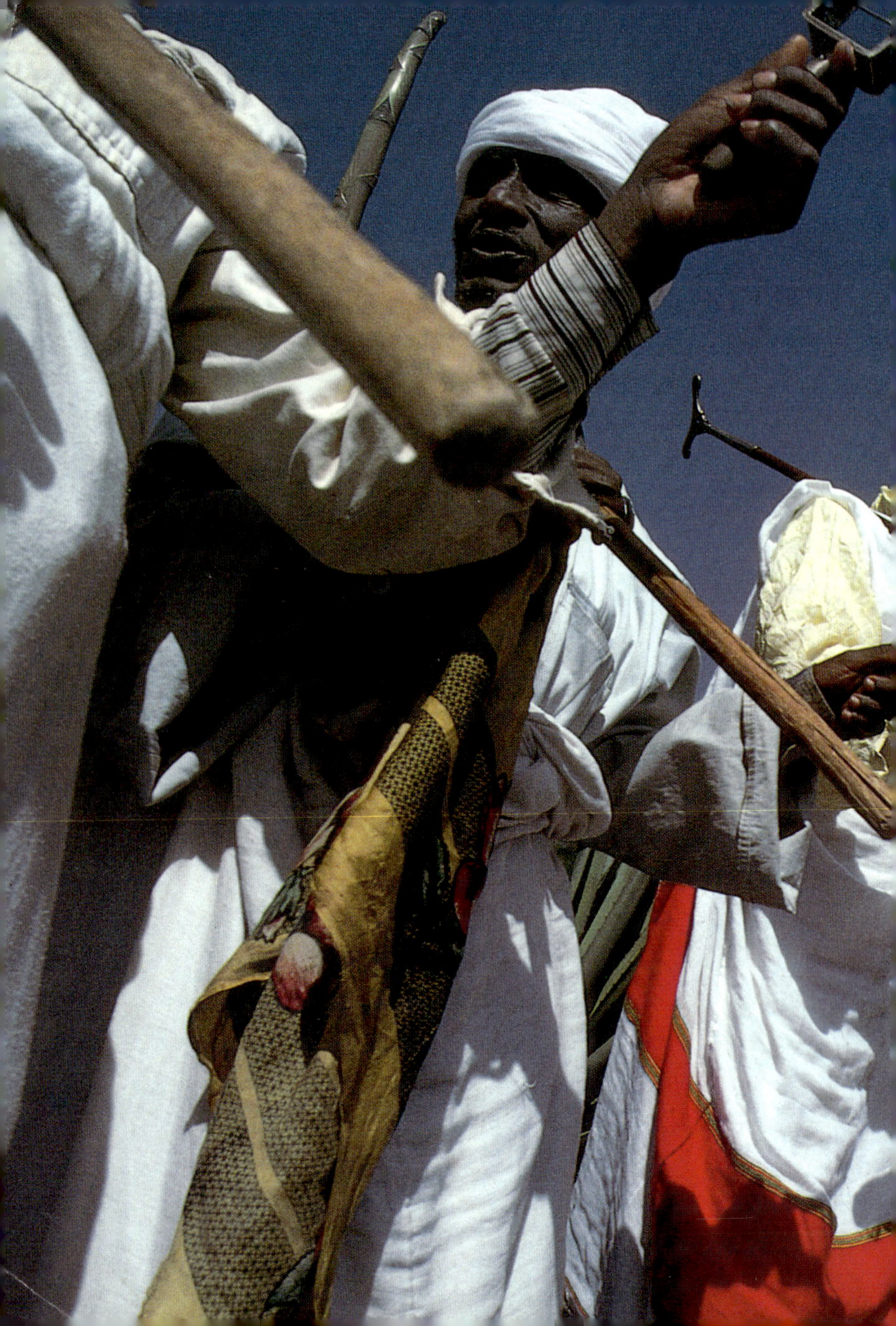

Discovering ETHIOPIA

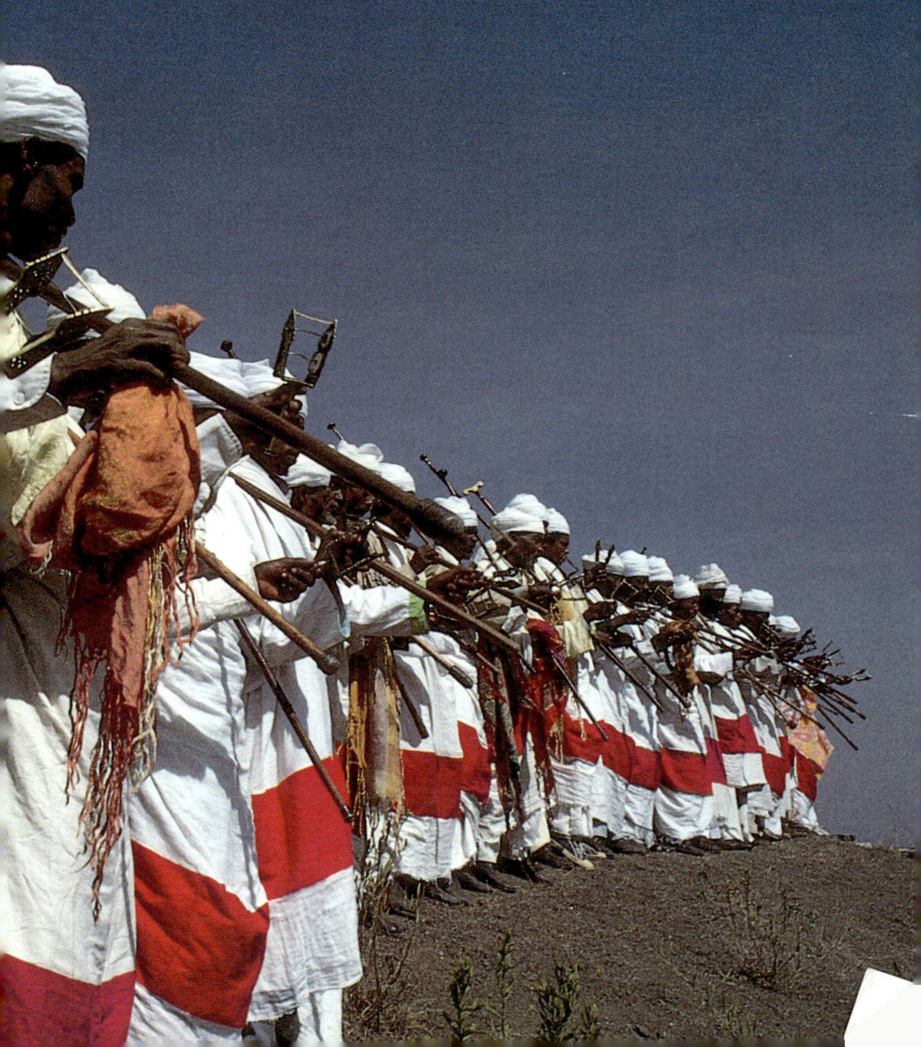

Revised edition published 1997 by
Camerapix Publishers Limited

First published 1983

This book was designed and produced by
Camerapix Publishers Limited,
PO Box 45048,
Nairobi, Kenya
ISBN 1 874041 84 9

Photography by Duncan Willetts, except on pages 31, 50, 74 (top) 106 (top) and 111, where pictures are by Kazuyoshi Nomachi.
Front cover, all photographs on page 18 and the lower left picture on page 19 are by Angela Fisher and Carol Beckwith.

Revised design by Harinder Kalsi and Calvin McKenzie.
Revised editing and production by Brian Tetley and Rukhsana Haq.

Colour Separation by Universal Graphics Pte Ltd
Printed by UIC Printing & Packaging Pte Ltd
(Singapore).

Contents

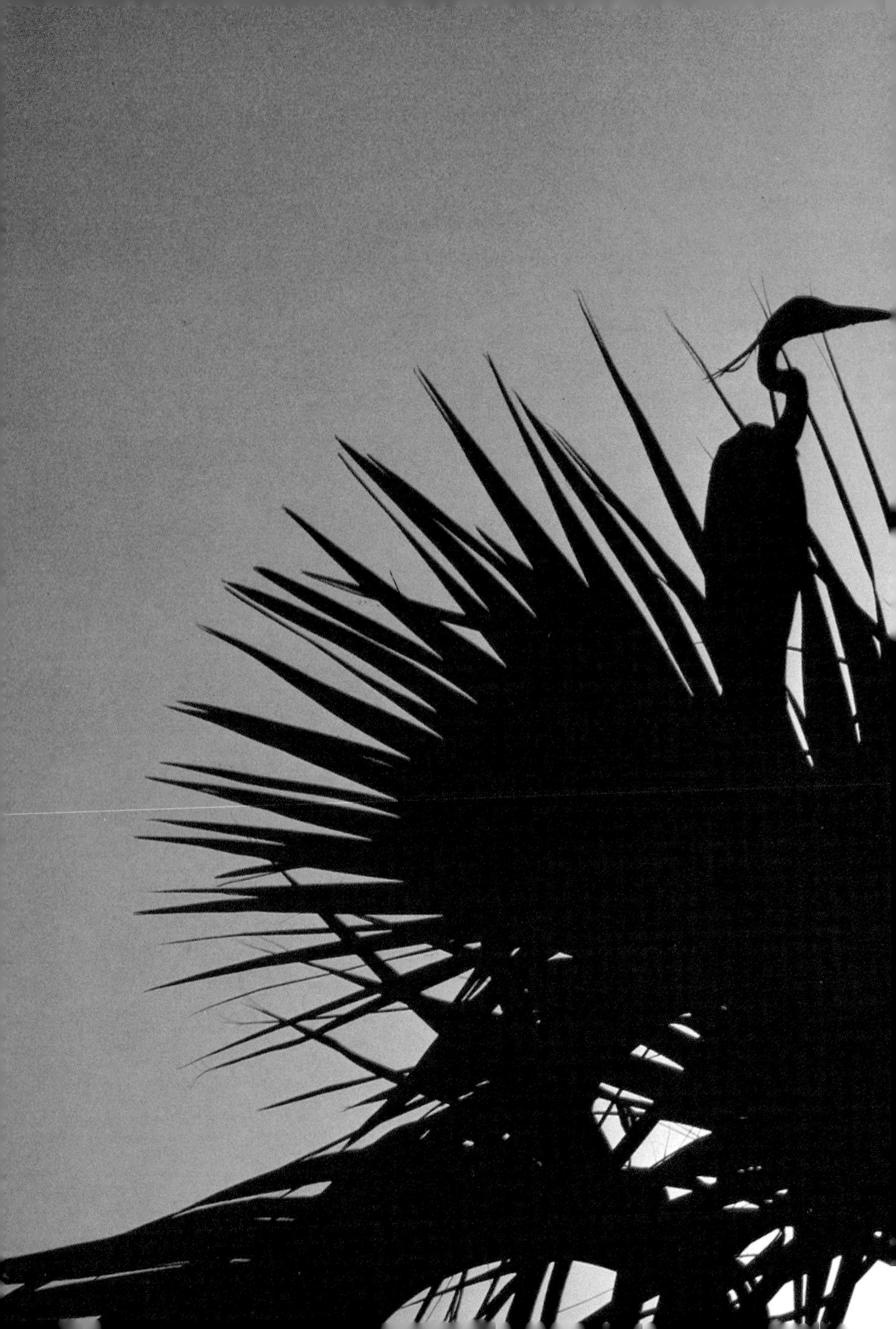

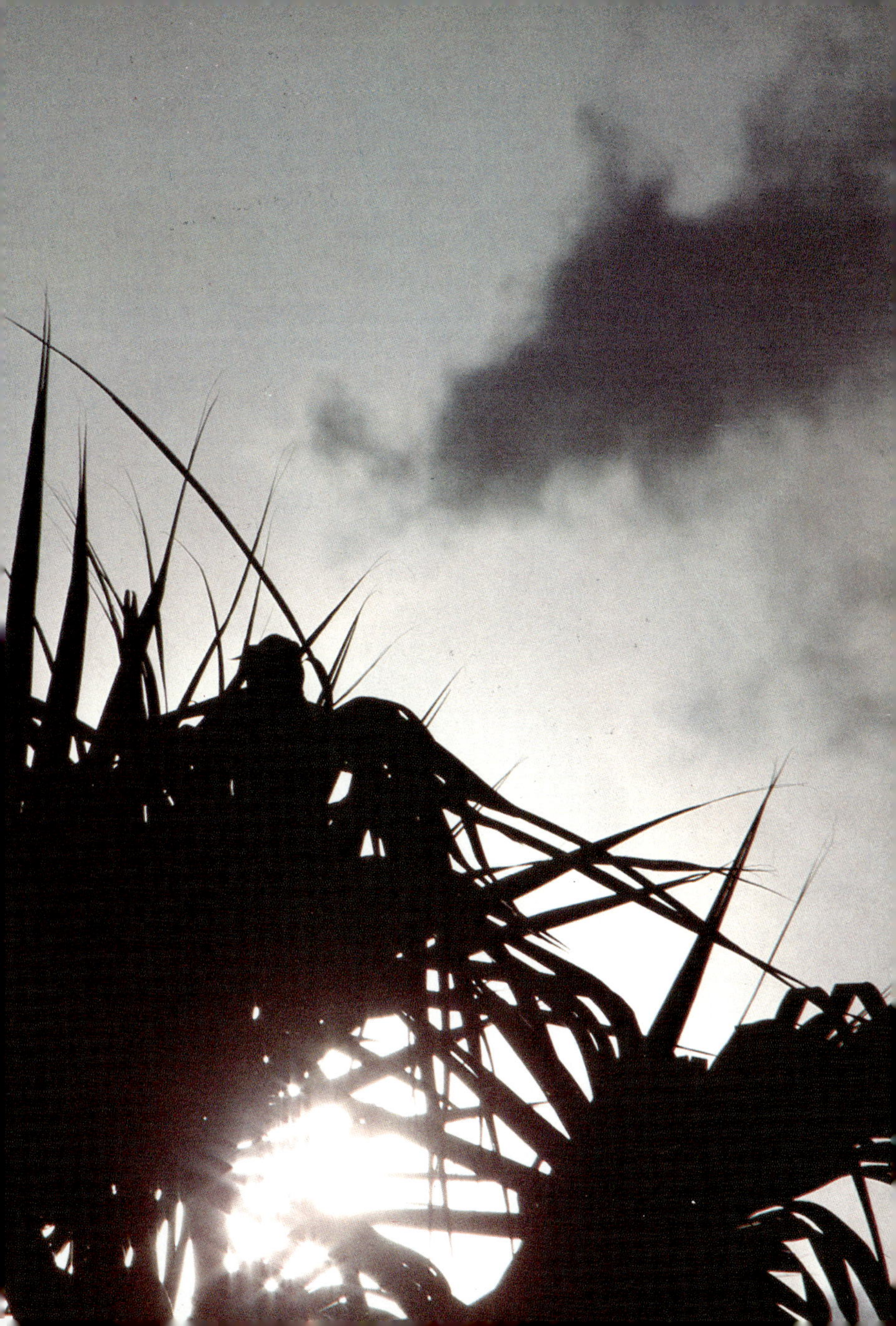

Chapter 4 · Nature and Wildlife

Chapter 5 · Towns and Cities to Visit

Chapter 6 · Useful Tips and Guidelines

Overleaf: The Dallol Depression in north-east Ethiopia, where sulphur stains the dazzling salt beds.

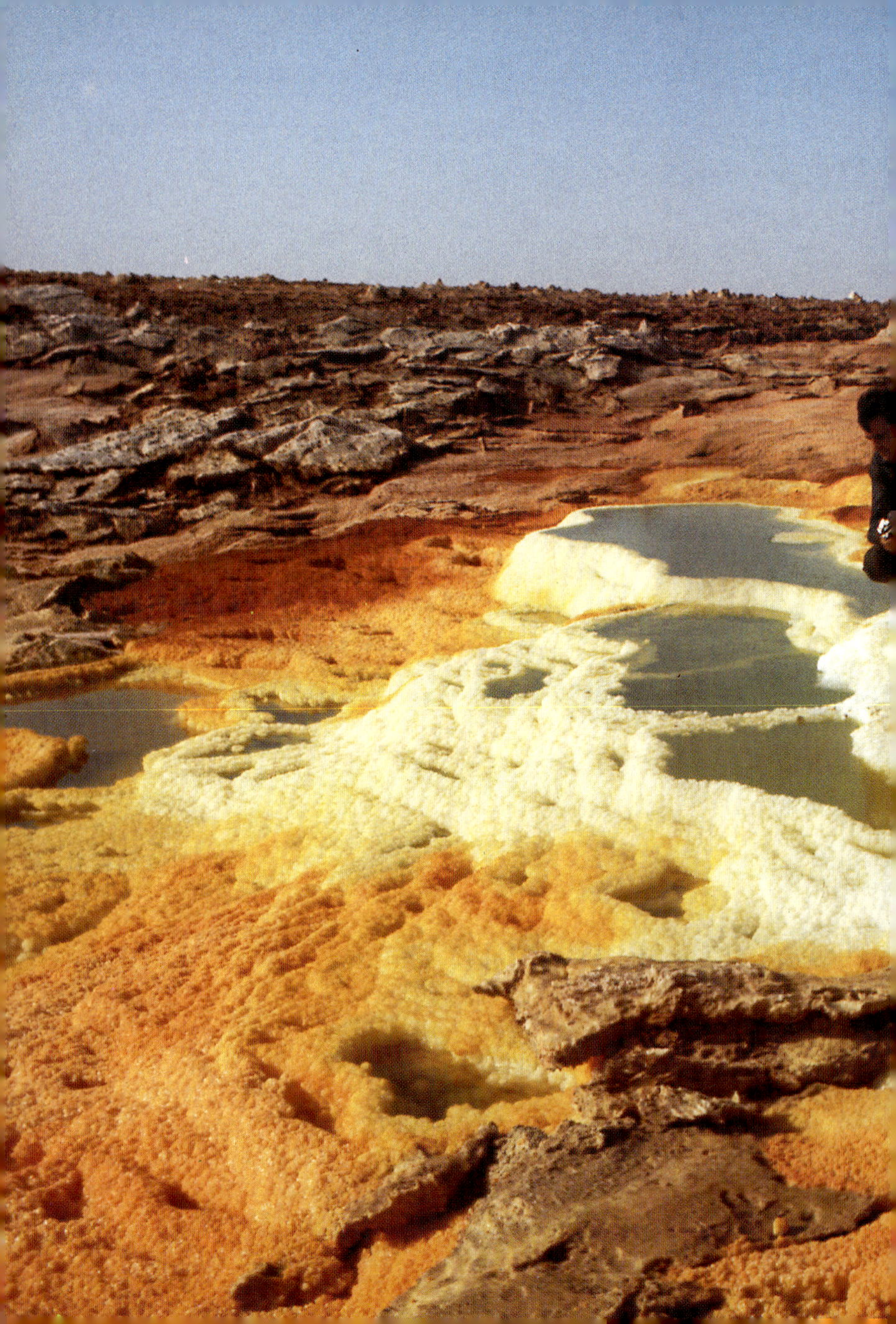

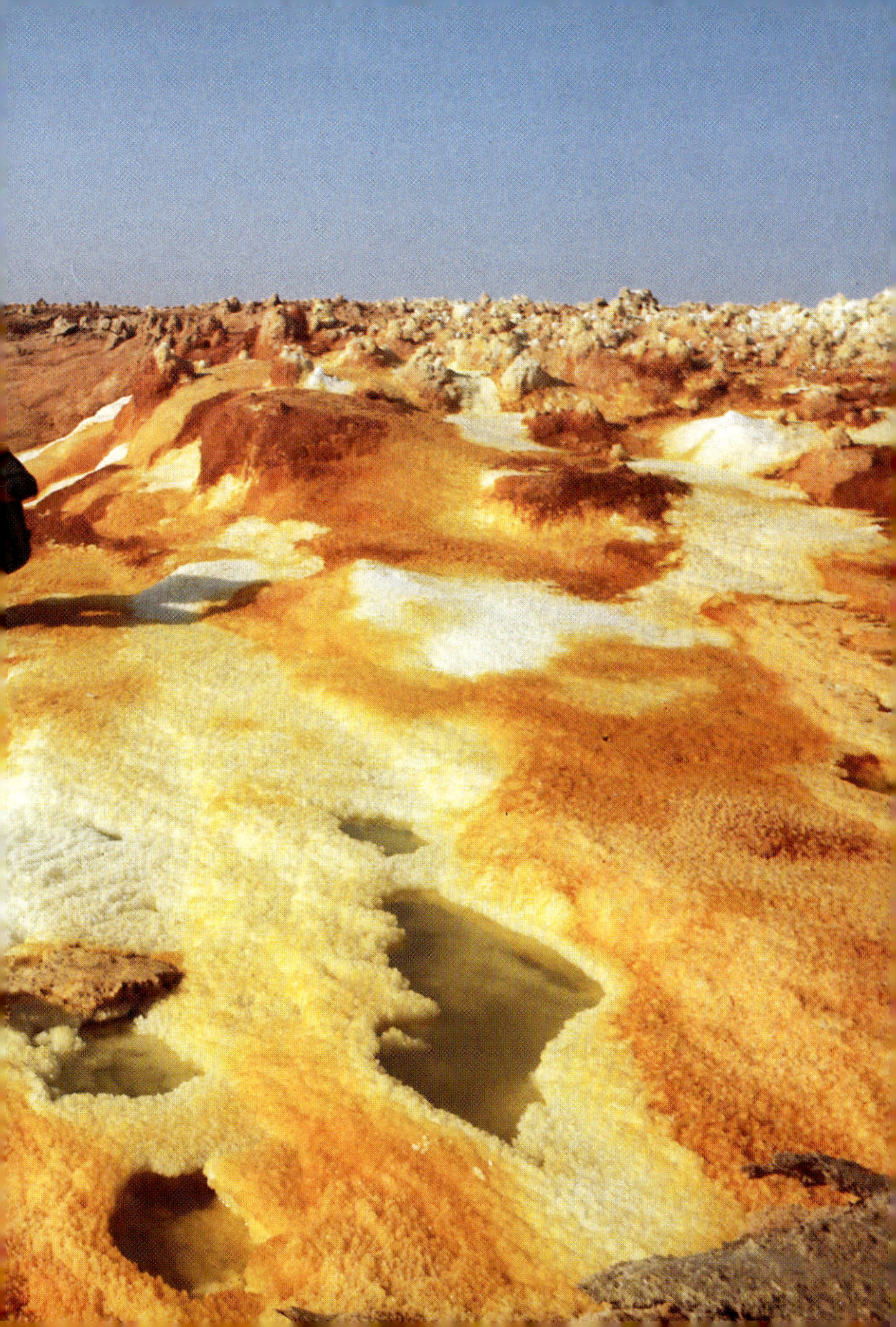

Chapter 1 · Land and People

Ethiopia is situated between 4° and 18° north of the Equator in eastern Africa. It is a ruggedly mountainous country enjoying a generally temperate climate throughout the year. Bordered by the Sudan, Kenya, Somalia, Eritrea and Djibouti, is the tenth largest country in Africa. Ethiopia has an area of 1,112,000 square kilometres. It is twice the size of Kenya, of France or of Texas. With a population of 55 million people, population density is highest in the fertile central highlands. At present only 10.4 per cent of the country is under any form of cultivation, although 68.8 per cent of the land area is deemed to be arable.

GEOGRAPHY

The central area of Ethiopia is a vast highland region of faulted volcanic rocks thrown up during the Tertiary Period of geological time over 20 million years ago when the great Rift Valley started to open. This huge and dramatic scar on the face of the earth in fact extends from Lebanon through the Red Sea, down the Danakil Depression and onwards to form the valleys of Ethiopia, Kenya and Tanzania before terminating in Mozambique.

The Ethiopian highlands alone cover an area roughly the size of France, and form a well-watered, temperate world of their own at between 1,500 and 4,700 metres surrounded by burning, inhospitable, lowland deserts where only the most determined can live with any semblance of success.

The highland escarpment, inhabited by the bulk of the Ethiopian population, is steep in the north, and has been denuded of soil by the silt carried away each year by the Blue Nile — the soil upon which Egypt's agriculture has prospered. The Simien Mountains — the Roof of Africa — rise to over

Below: Giant gorges and towering peaks of the Simien Mountains.

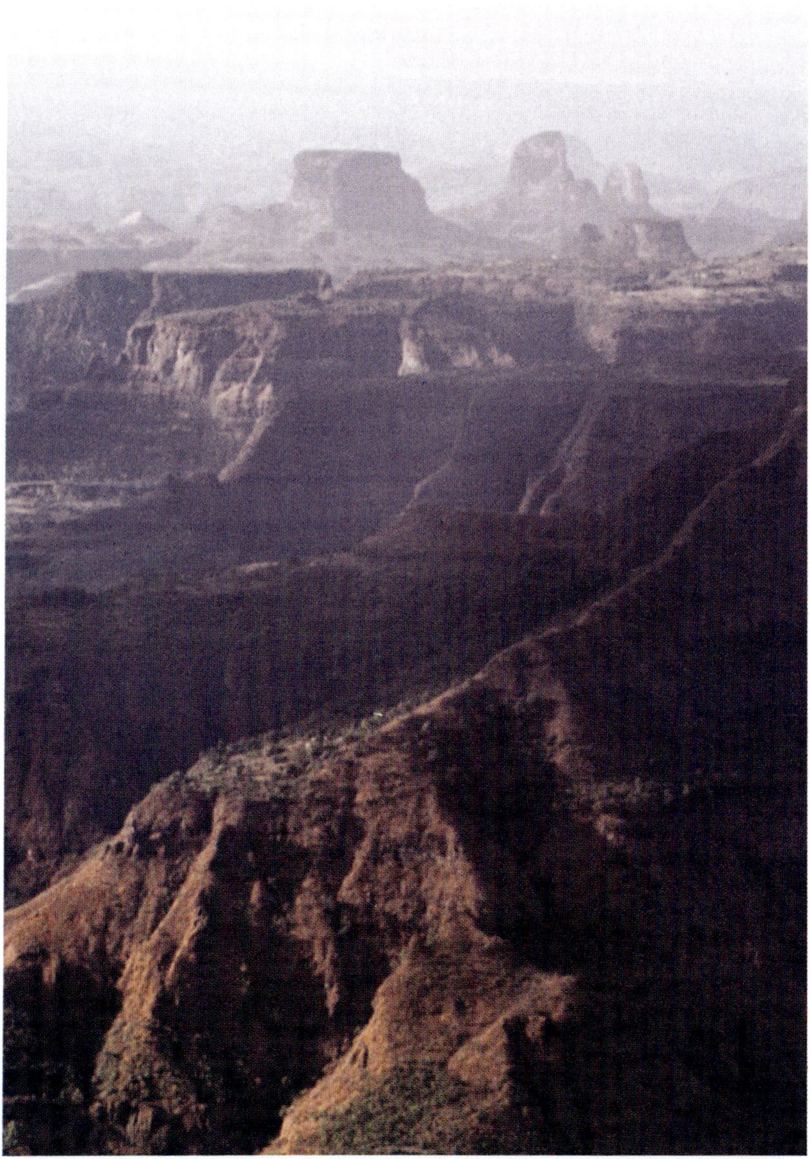

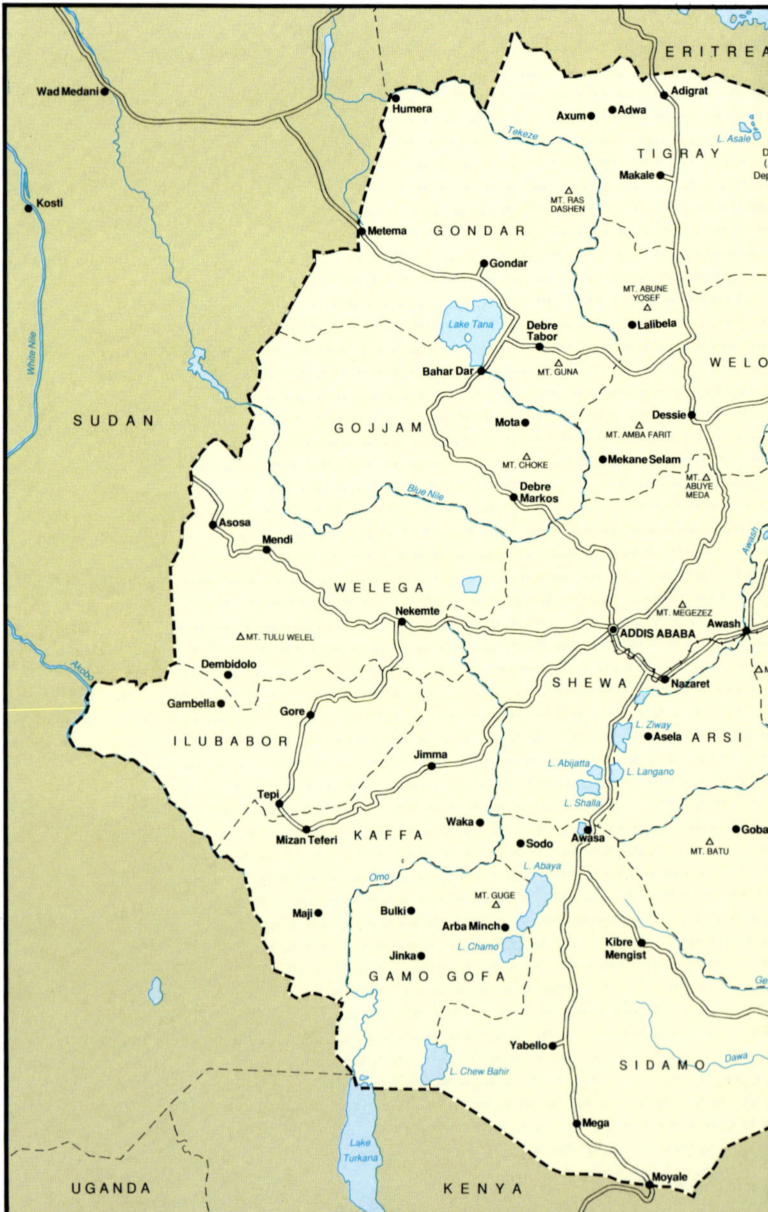
ERITREA
Wad Medani
Humera
Adigrat
Axum
Adwa
Tekeze
L. Asale
TIGRAY
Makale
Kosti
MT. RAS DASHEN
Metema
GONDAR
Gondar
MT. ABUNE YOSEF
Lalibela
Lake Tana
Debre Tabor
WELO
White Nile
Bahar Dar
MT. GUNA
Dessie
SUDAN
GOJJAM
Mota
MT. AMBA FARIT
Mekane Selam
MT. CHOKE
MT. ABUYE MEDA
Blue Nile
Debre Markos
Asosa
Mendi
Awash
WELEGA
MT. MEGEZEZ
Nekemte
Awash
ADDIS ABABA
MT. TULU WELEL
Akobo
Dembidolo
SHEWA
Nazaret
Gambella
Gore
L. Ziway
Asela
ARSI
ILUBABOR
Jimma
L. Abijatta
L. Langano
L. Shalla
Tepi
Waka
Goba
Mizan Teferi
KAFFA
Sodo
Awasa
MT. BATU
Omo
L. Abaya
MT. GUGE
Maji
Bulki
Arba Minch
Kibre Mengist
L. Chamo
Jinka
GAMO GOFA
Genale
Yabello
SIDAMO
Dawa
L. Chew Bahir
Mega
Lake Turkana
Moyale
UGANDA
KENYA

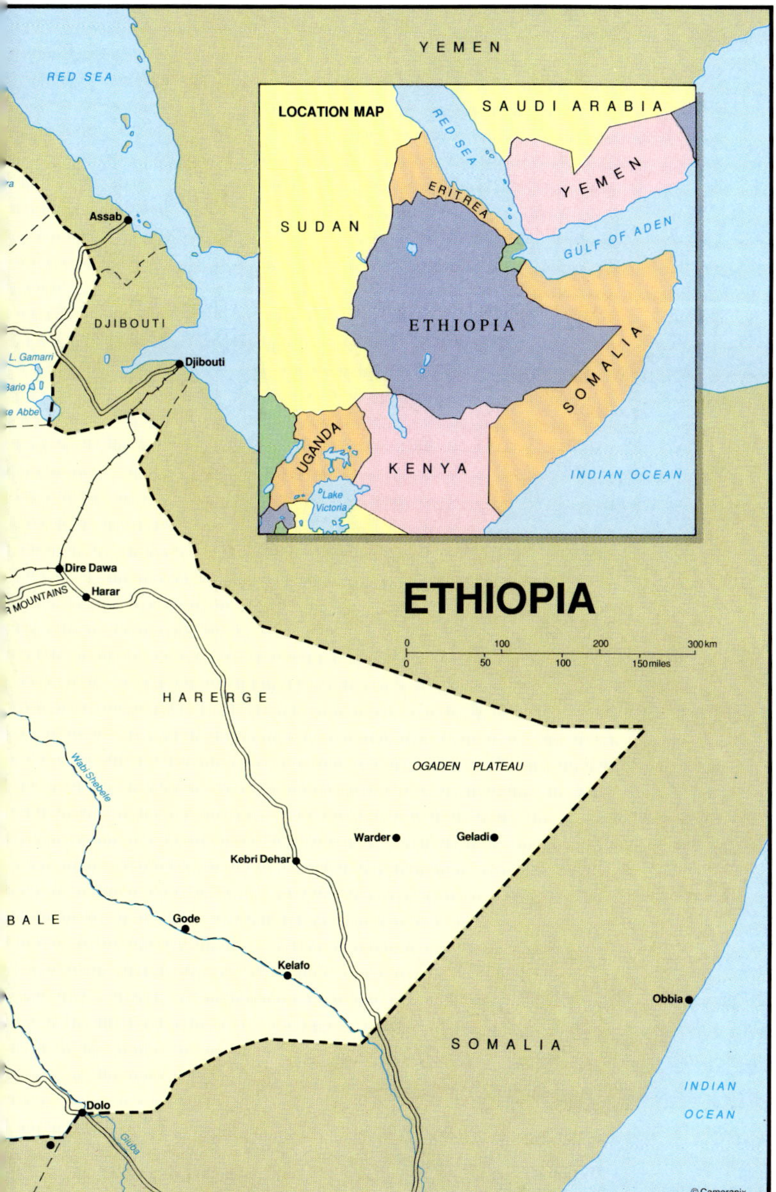

YEMEN
RED SEA
LOCATION MAP
SAUDI ARABIA
RED SEA
YEMEN
ERITREA
SUDAN
GULF OF ADEN
ETHIOPIA
SOMALIA
UGANDA
KENYA
INDIAN OCEAN
Lake Victoria
Assab
DJIBOUTI
Djibouti
L. Gamarri
Dire Dawa
Harar
MOUNTAINS
ETHIOPIA
0 100 200 300 km
0 50 100 150 miles
HARERGE
Wabi Shebele
OGADEN PLATEAU
Warder
Geladi
Kebri Dehar
BALE
Gode
Kelafo
Obbia
SOMALIA
INDIAN OCEAN
Dolo
Giuba
© Camerapix

4,000 metres, and the highest point is Ras Deshen (4,453 metres). The Danakil basin, lying between the highlands and Eritrea, contains, by contrast, an extensive and deep depression 130 metres below sea-level where some of the highest temperatures on earth have been recorded. This area was once part of the sea-bed and yields rock salt in apparently limitless quantities. The deposits at Lake Abbe are thought to be between 3,000 metres and 4,500 metres deep.

To the south the land drops away gently and the agricultural potential is rich. Parts of the Sidamo highlands, with rolling grassland and neat hilltop copses, look as if they belong not to Africa at all, but to some other, more northern, continent. Despite the rich greenery of the south, it is an anomaly of the Ethiopian environment that the population is concentrated more densely in the north.

LANDMARKS

Ethiopia is a land of stunning natural beauty and her mountains, lakes, and rivers have many fascinating features. There are some 25 mountains in central and northern Ethiopia over 4,000 metres high; 60 mountains are over 3,000 metres high. Ras Deshen, in the Gondar region, is the fourth highest mountain in Africa.

Ethiopia's most famous river is the Blue Nile, also known as the Abbay. Its total length to its junction with the White Nile in Khartoum is 1,450 kilometres, 800 kilometres of which are inside Ethiopia. Travellers revere the Abbay as one of the twin sources of the mighty Nile; but the river also has immense hydroelectric potential which gives it a direct economic importance to Ethiopia, over and above its significance as a tourist attraction.

Other important rivers in Ethiopia are the Wabi Shebele, Genale, Awash, Omo, Tekeze, Mereb, Baro and Angereb. The Awash, the longest river inside Ethiopia, is a source of great agro-industrial wealth and hydroelectric power. Feasibility studies have been carried out on the other rivers such as the Wabi Shebele (which runs for 1,000 kilometres inside Ethiopia) for irrigation and power purposes. Because of the threat of malaria, the banks of most Ethiopian rivers are not heavily settled.

There are seven natural lakes and one large man-made reservoir (Koka) in the Rift Valley, situated in warm lowland areas, generally below 1,600 metres. Fishing, boating, and bird-watching make these beautiful stretches of water attractive to tourists. Lake Tana, in the Gondar region (not part of the Rift Valley), is Ethiopia's largest lake, with an area of 3,600 square kilometres. Lake Abaya, 1,160 kilometres, is the second largest. Others include Lake Chamo (551 square kilometres), Lake Ziway (434 square kilometres) and Lake Shala (409 square kilometres). Lake Shala reaches a depth of 250 metres. The depths of other lakes vary from four to 85 metres.

CLIMATE

Weather conditions in Ethiopia are determined by the physical nature of the country and by its situation close to the Indian Ocean. Throughout the year it is warm and pleasant in the low-lying areas and cool and bracing in the central highlands. There are two principal seasons: rainy from June through October; relatively dry for the rest of the year. Meteorological conditions vary according to the altitude. In some areas in the central highlands, there is a month-long season of 'little rains'

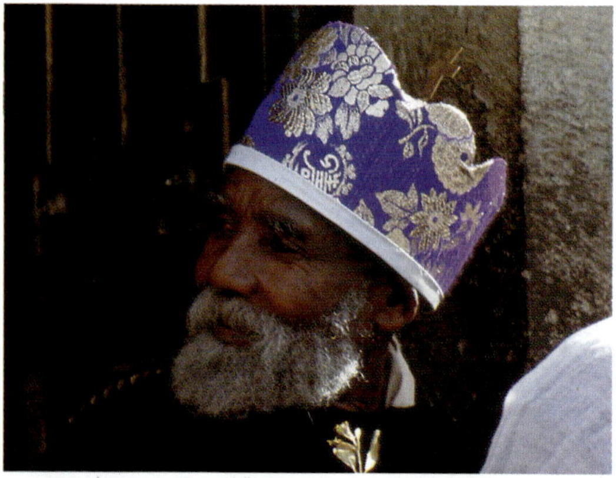
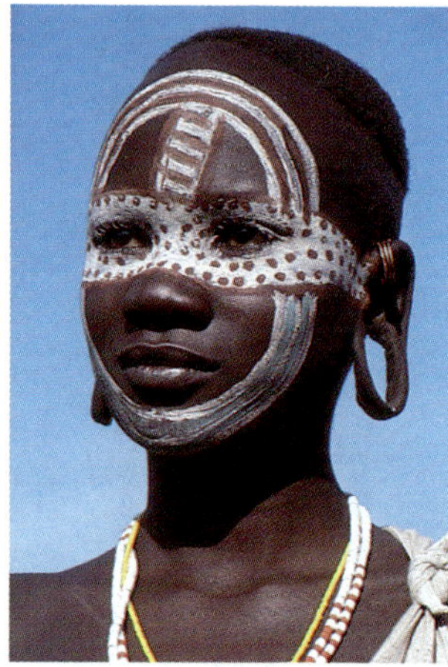
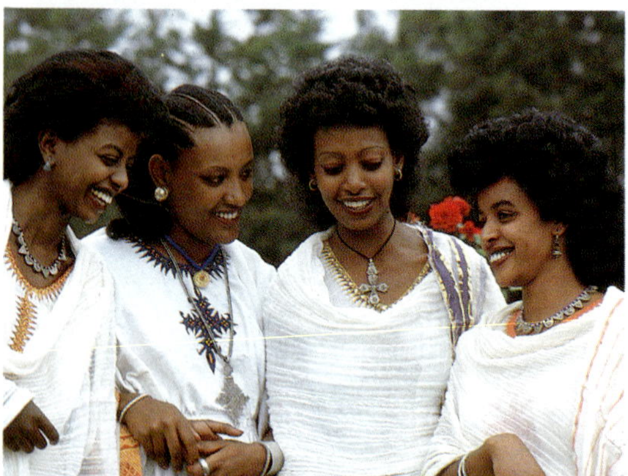
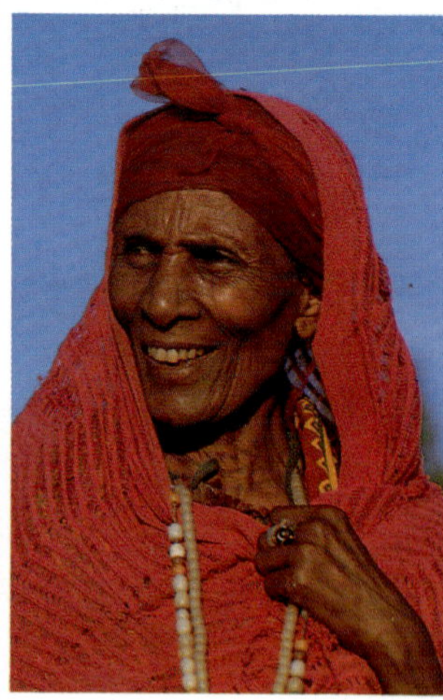
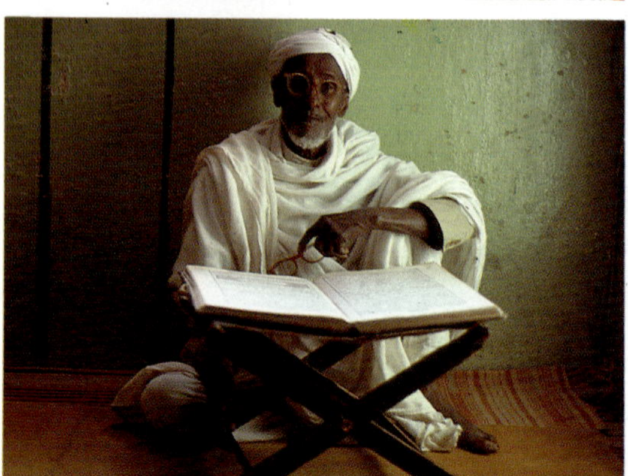

A mosaic of Ethiopian peoples. The country has more than 80 different languages and great cultural diversity.

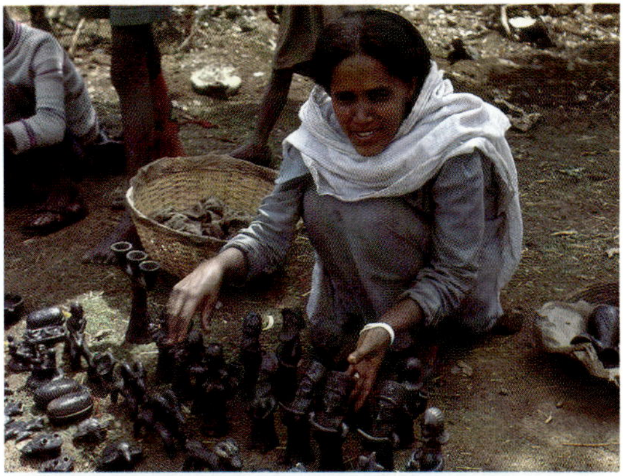

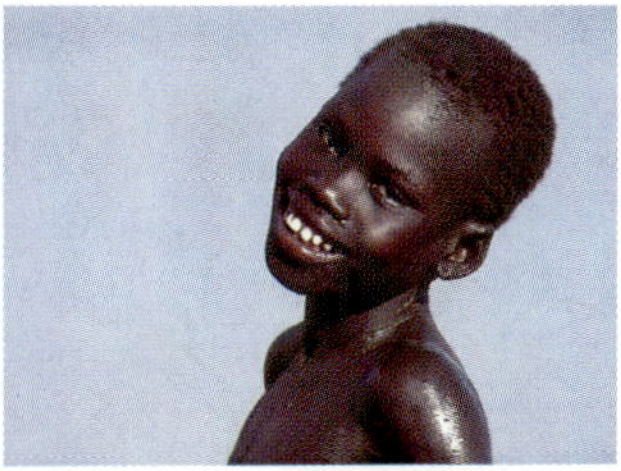

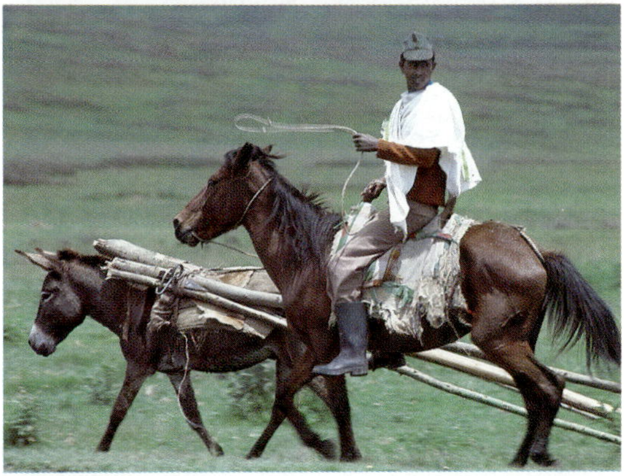

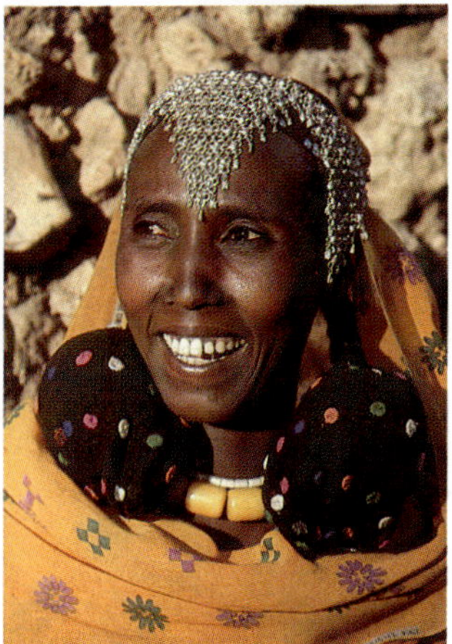

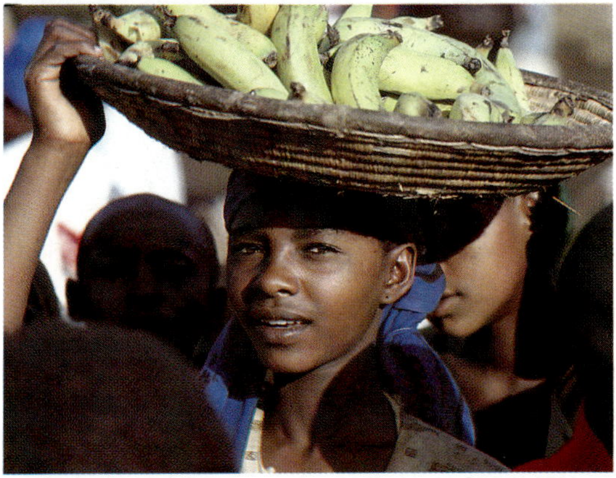

early in the year. The average temperature during the hottest season is 18 C° falling to 14 C° in the rainy season.

The amount of rainfall varies from place to place. However, in most parts of the central highlands the annual average is well over 1,000mm. Typical average rainfall is 1,150mm in Addis Ababa, 1,230 in Dessie, 640 in Dire Dawa, 1,240 in Gambella, 1,250 in Gondar, 900 in Harar, 1,500 in Jimma, and 670 in Neghellie (these figures based on a three-year survey).

The wettest months for the central highlands are July and August, while November and December have the coldest nights. During the nights of the coldest months the temperature often drops to around freezing point. Humidity varies between 50 per cent and 80 per cent throughout the year. The Ethiopian climate is generally Mediterranean in character.

PEOPLE AND LANGUAGES

It is not without reason that the great historian, Conti-Rossini, characterised Ethiopia as a rich cultural mosaic. There are over 80 languages and dialects in Ethiopia and as many cultural variations.

In the northernmost highlands are to be found speakers of Tigre, a Semitic language closely linked to the ancient Ge'ez now surviving only in church liturgy and literature. In the Tigray region, where Axum is found, another Semitic language, Tigrinya, is spoken. The heartland of Ethiopia is the homeland of Amharic, the official Ge'ez language, also derived from Ge'ez. Further south, Guraginya, a Semitic language, is spoken by a numerically small ethnic group of Hamitic origin.

To the east and south are the Cushitic-speaking peoples: the Oromos the Afars and the Somalis. The linked Sidama group of languages are spoken in the south-east. Although the various Oromo clans have remained socially distinct, their common culture is a fascinating feature of their lives. This kind of unity in diversity is one of the special characteristics of Ethiopia today.

To the far west and south-west, Ethiopia's Nilotic peoples are found: the Nuer and the Anuak living near Gambella and other scattered groups further south. Each has its own distinctive language and culture.

Also found in Ethiopia are a number of small communities whose languages and cultures are connected to specific aspects of the country's long history. One such group is the Falasha, now living in the Gondar region whose culture reflects Ethiopia's early links with Judaic Palestine. Ethiopians are generally considered to be a courteous and hospitable people. They were known to Homer as the "blameless race" with whom the gods dined. Ethiopians are proud and patriotic. Fine soldiers, they have been known for their bravery and achievements since ancient times.

RELIGIONS

Ethiopian culture and tradition have been much influenced by both Christian and Muslim religions. The Amharas and Tigres are predominantly Christian and adhere to the Orthodox Church. The Oromos, the largest ethnic group in the country (who appeared in central Ethiopia in the 16th century), are more mixed, with Christian, Muslim and pagan communities.

LIFESTYLES

In their political structures the different peoples of Ethiopia have evolved their own distinct but equally fascinating solutions to the age-old problems of individual freedom and

Below: Young girl of Dire Dawa shows off her jewellery, bracelets and beads.

Right: Colourful umbrellas are an important part of the religious symbolism employed in Ethiopia

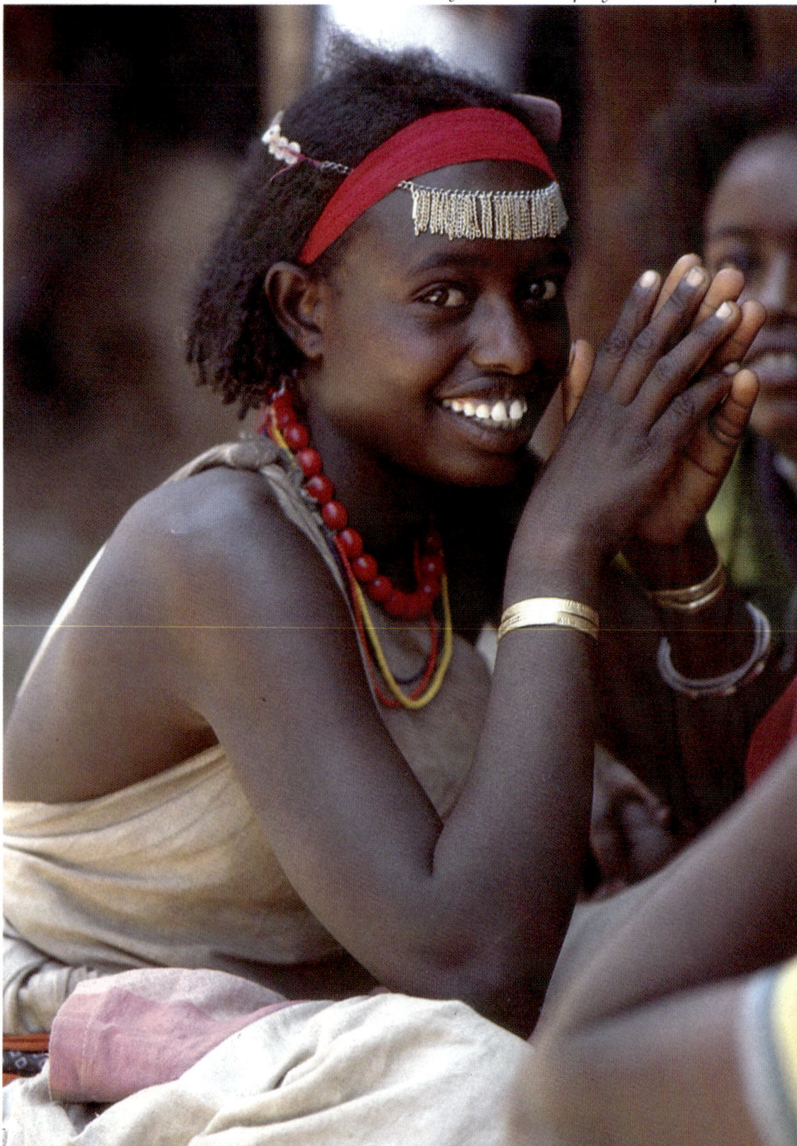

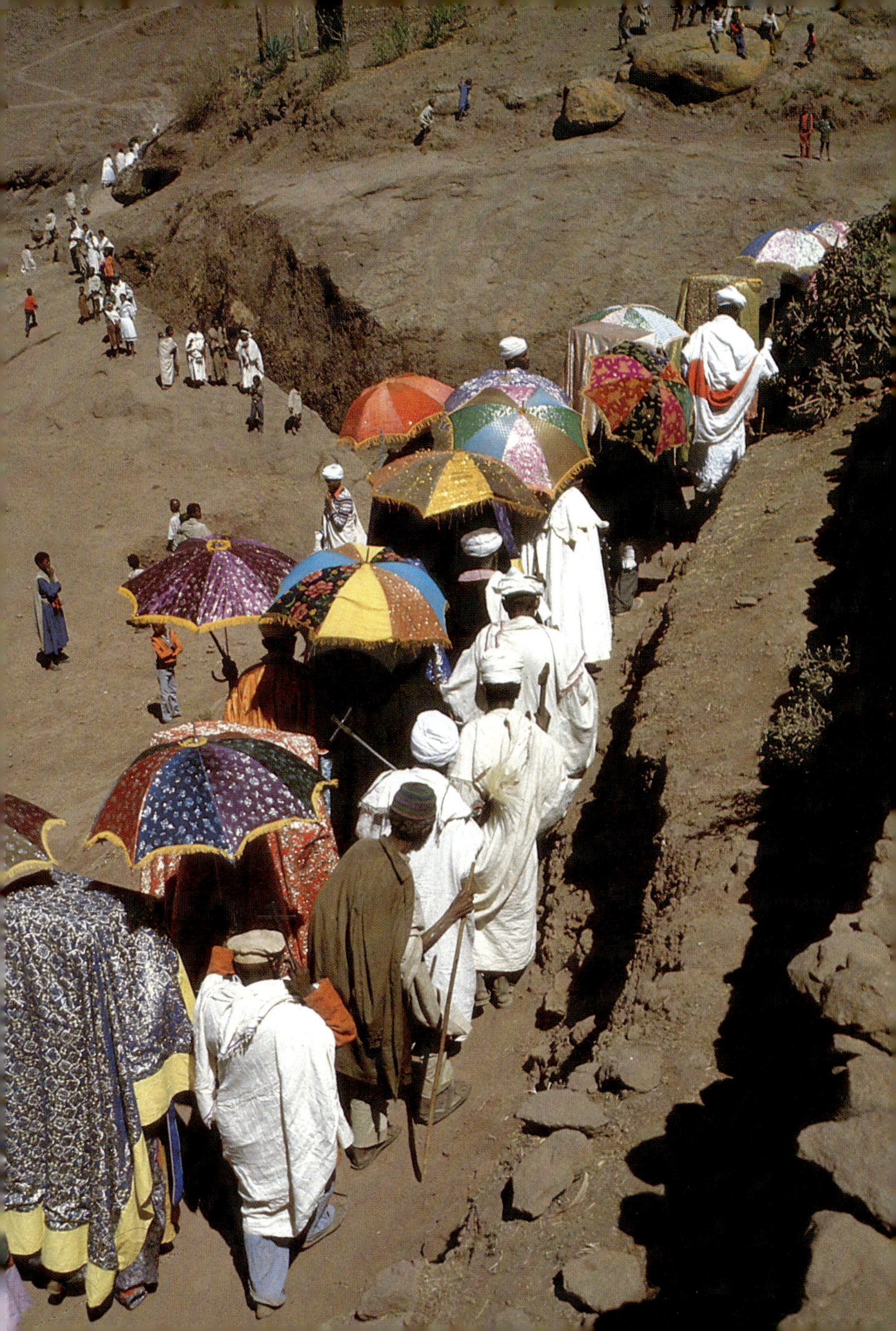

social control. The Borena in the south, along the border with Kenya, used to run an almost perfect form of 'presidential' government. Every eight years an *Aba Gada* (father of the Gada, or the age-group system) was elected who would administer the tribe by travelling round Borena territory according to a set route and routine throughout his entire term of office, spending a month at each stop.

Like all the 80 nationalities of the country, the Adares, the Afars and the Ethiopian Somalis of Harerge have their own distinct ways of life. In the hotter lowlands that these people inhabit, the donkey and the mule give way to the camel as the principal beast of burden, and Islam is the predominant religion.

Ethiopia is first in Africa in her livestock population. Nearly 90 per cent of all Ethiopians are engaged in farming and cattle-raising and live in the countryside.

Be they the Afar or the ethnic Somali of the Danakil and the Ogaden, the Anuak of the south-west, or the Borena along the border with Kenya, the peripheral inhabitants of Ethiopia lead a nomadic and pastoral way of life. The central highlands by contrast, have supported farming communities for thousands of years, and the Christian highland peoples have followed a biblical, moral and civic code of behaviour for over 16 centuries. Despite the predominance of Christianity in these regions, small islands of Islamic settlement are also found.

Farmers in the Ethiopian highlands grow cereals, pulses and oilseeds. Their staple food, *injera,* is made from *teff (Eragrostis Abyssinica)* which is a tiny grain related to millet and indigenous to Ethiopia.

The Konso, who inhabit mountainous terrain in Gamo Gofa state, have practised the technique of terraced agriculture for

Overleaf: An important Islamic shrine, the Sof Omar caves situated in the eastern Bale are the site of a major festival each year in the month of May.

over 400 years. The result is an amazing picturesque landscape with the green intricacy of terraces merging into the contours of the hillsides.

The Gurage have evolved a virtually famine-proof way of life based on cultivation of the versatile *enset* plant (false banana), which they use for purposes ranging from food to the construction of large spacious houses.

The Dorze are famous for their craftsmanship in weaving and for their fascinating funeral rituals.

The gentle folk of Gambella lead a truly pastoral existence with seasonal sorghum planting and fishing carried out along the Baro River. This relatively large river plays a central role in the life of the Nuer and the Anuak in much the same way as the Omo affects the lives of the Mursi, the Karo and the Galeb.

COSTUMES

The costumes of the Ethiopian people are as varied and interesting as the population itself, reflecting ancient and modern trends in decoration; the fanciful as well as the practical. A love of ornamentation ruled by a natural affinity for beauty leads Ethiopians to adorn themselves in often memorably dramatic fashions.

Timeless symbols such as the cross and lion's mane have long been used in decoration. Tattooing of the forehead, cheeks, neck and hands, and elaborate traditional coiffure, though no longer the rule with sophisticated city dwellers, are still seen everywhere among the rural folk.

A profusion of jewellery is an integral part of national dress, whether crafted by skilled gold- and silversmiths, or by village artisans working with cowrie shells, base metals and colourful beads. And rain or shine, richly ornamented umbrellas,

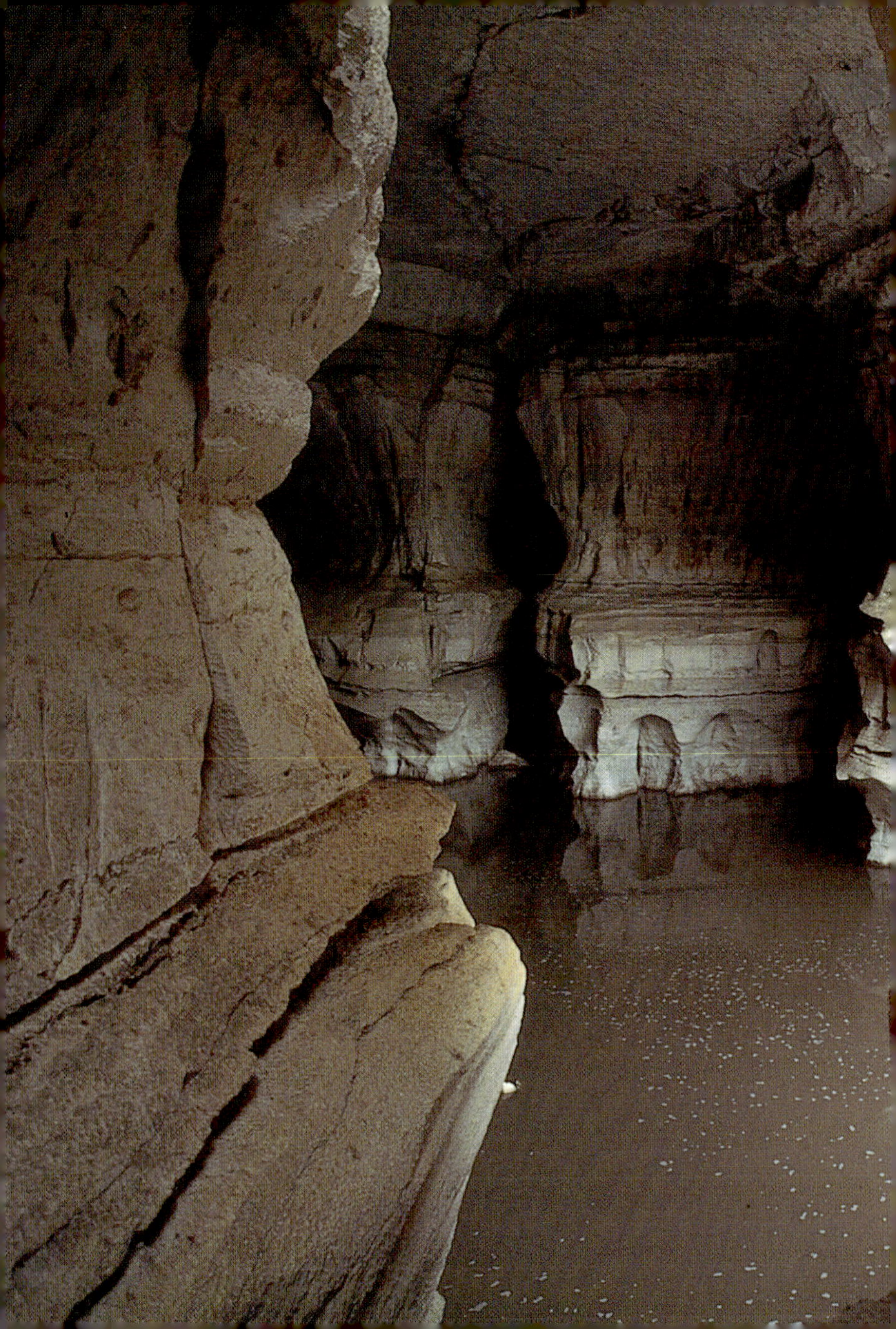

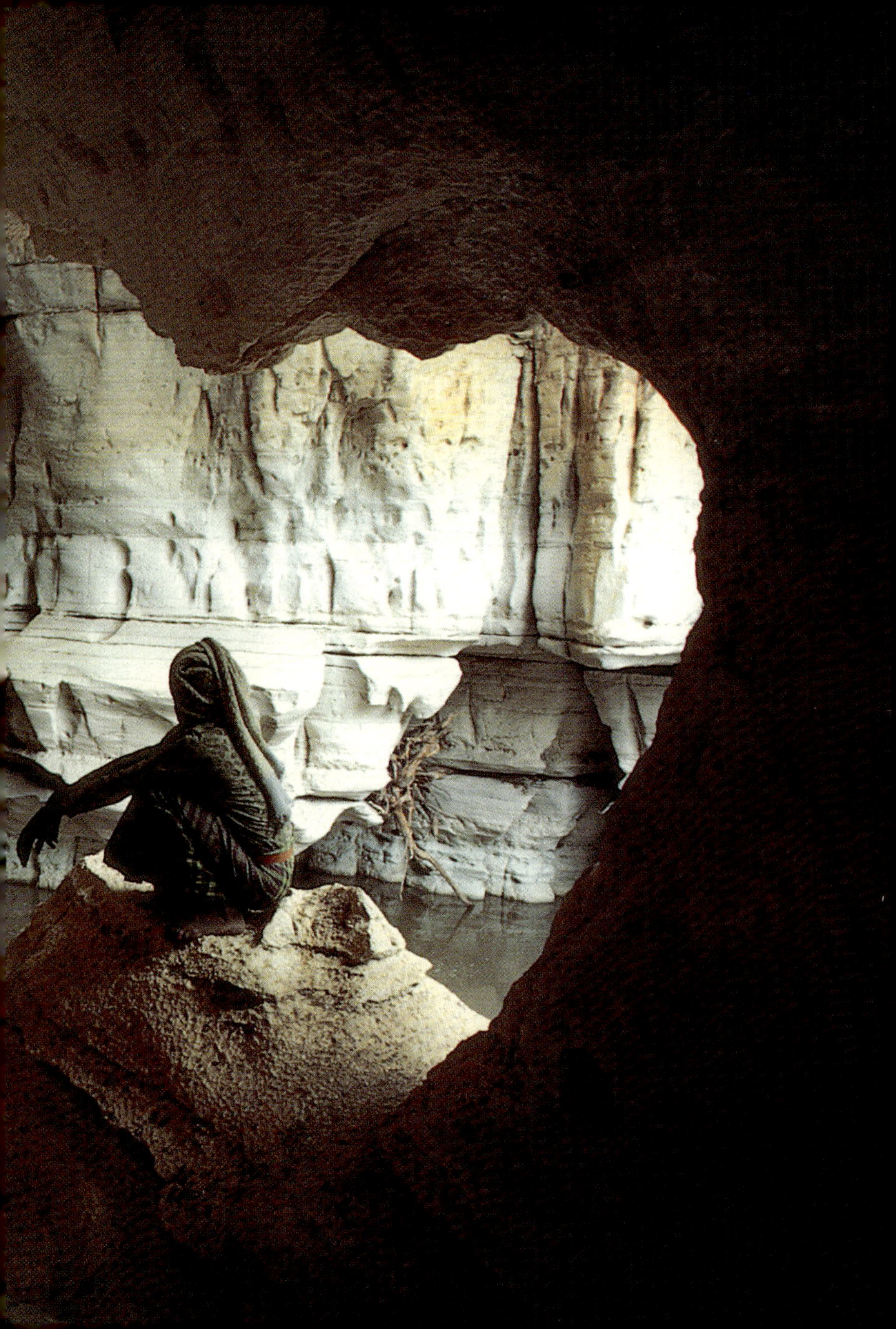

gorgeous in colour, are held above the heads of priests and deacons during church services. In their dress, as in other areas of cultural and religious tradition, the Ethiopians participate in a heritage that is lively, colourful and unique. One delight awaiting the visitor is the ever-changing pageant of costumes that will pass before them as they walk through the cities or drive about the countryside, as they witness a religious ceremony or take part in public celebrations.

Generally speaking, the basic costume of highland Ethiopia is the *shamma,* a loose flowing garment often worn in addition to skirts, skirts and trousers. In the streets of Addis Ababa the traveller will see the shamma in all its permutations. Other common items of apparel include the *netela* (single-sheet), a light cotton shawl; the *kutta,* a heavier version of the netela; the gabi, a course blanket-like cotton cloth worn for warmth; and the *burnous,* or black cloak. The *kemis* is a full-length embroidered dress with an embroidered hemline, worn by women.

In the hot lowlands Ethiopians often wear little or nothing above the waist. They wear a leather skirt or a *shirit,* a piece of cotton cloth wound around the waist and coming down the calf.

FESTIVALS

The bright blue sky and the bracing highland air supplant the gloom of the season of thunder and lightning. The torrential rains, the hail storms and the muddy floods subside and the ground firms up, coming alive again with greenery, the spectacle of flowers, and with ripe crops filling the air with sweet effervescence. This is *Tseday,* the Ethiopian season of spring, and a very delightful time to see the countryside. Maskaram First (11 September) is New Year's Day, the harbinger of the harvest season, merry-making and marriage.

But perhaps the most unusual of Ethiopia's many festivals are those of Kulubi Gabriel, Gishen Mariam, Sheikh Hussein and Sof Omar. Vast crowds turn up each year to pray for a cure, a baby, some special grace, or to give thanks for prayers already fulfilled. St Mary's Churches at Axum and Lalibela have their own big annual religious festivals taking place in January and during Ethiopian Christmas respectively.

The second important festival is *Meskal,* on 27 September, when Ethiopians commemorate the finding of the True Cross by St Helena, the wife of Constantine the Great. Huge bonfires are lit all over the country on the eve of Meskal and dancing and feasting take place on the day itself. Meskal also marks the end of the big rains and the advent of the season of flowers.

On 19 January there is the feast of Epiphany, or *Timket,* probably Ethiopia's most celebrated festival — and certainly the easiest and the most convenient for outsiders to see and enjoy. On the eve of Timket, the holy *Tabot* (Ark of Covenant) of each church is brought to some central watering place where the following morning bishops, elders, and the clergy assemble in all their gorgeous costumes for all Christians of the neighbourhood to renew their vows and be sprinkled with holy water, after which the Tabots are borne in procession back to their various churches accompanied by their respective congregations.

Easter is the most solemn of the festivals. Its celebration is accompanied by the unique and sacred music and dance of the Church and by the most moving rituals during midnight Mass.

CALENDAR

Ethiopia still retains the Julian calendar, named after Julius Caesar, for whom it was devised by Alexandrian astronomers.

Opposite: The 12th century city of Lalibela, with its remarkable rock-hewn churches, is one of the best places in which to participate in the dramatic Timket *festival.*

The year is divided into 12 months of 30 days each and a 13th month of five or six days (hence the tourism promotion slogan "13 months of sunshine"). Taking for its starting point the Birth of Christ — and owing to differences of opinion over the date — the Ethiopian calendar is seven years and eight months behind the Gregorian calendar, Ethiopian Christmas Day is on 7 January of the Gregorian calendar, while Ethiopian Easter coincides with Gregorian Easter once every four years.

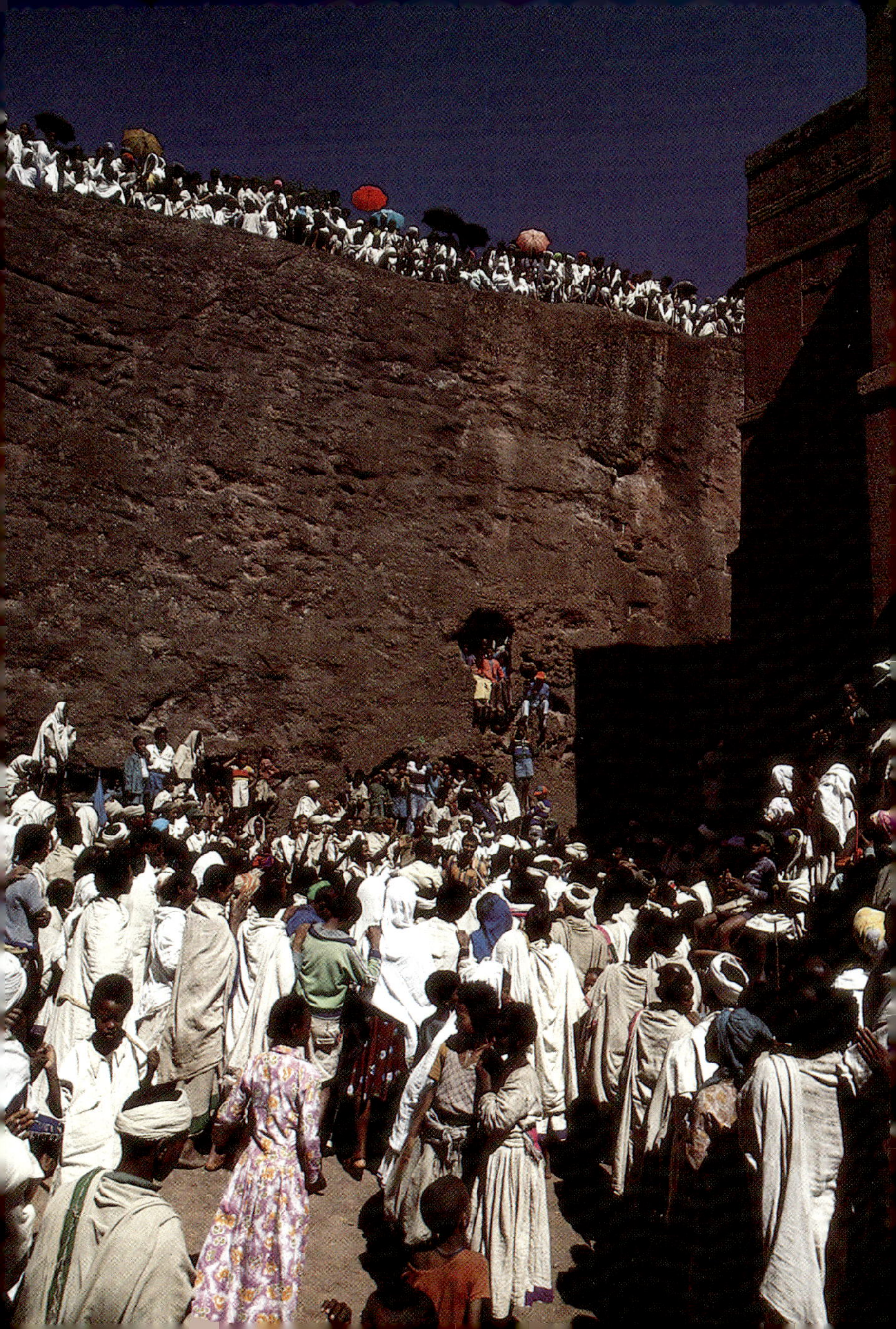

Chapter 2 · History

Ethiopia may well be the true 'Cradle of mankind', since the fossilised remains of man's oldest known ancestor, *Australopithecus Afarensis,* have been found here. Dating back at least 3.5 million years, the original find — nicknamed 'Lucy' — was made in 1974 at a site on the lower Awash River in north-east Ethiopia, and has since been supplemented by many other discoveries in the Omo River valley and elsewhere on the Awash. 'Lucy' was an upright-walking hominid, a metre tall, with a small brain and apelike features. Her teeth, as well as her legs and pelvic bones are, however, distinctly human. Her discovery rocked the world of palaeoanthropology because it proved that mankind's ancestors were at least a million years older than had hitherto been believed.

LEGEND AND ANCIENT HISTORY

Early tradition has it that Cush, one of the sons of Ham and a grandson of Noah, came to Ethiopia from Mesopotamia. Latter-day legend claims that Menilek I, the son born to Solomon by the Queen of Sheba, settled in Axum bringing with him the Ark of the Covenant from the Temple in Jerusalem to establish the dynasty which reigned — with only brief interruptions — until 1974. Ethiopia had, in fact, one of the world's longest uninterrupted monarchical lines.

Ethiopia's historical importance stemmed, in part, from her favourable location and terrain. The cool, celestial 'island' of ancient times was not only part of Africa but also lay on the edge of the Graeco-Roman world to which it was linked both by the Nile River system and the Red Sea. Ties of kinship, proximity, culture and trade also provided connections with the Indo-Persian-Arab races. Lying at the centre of these three cultural worlds and protected on the east by her inhospitable

Overleaf: The castle of King Fasiladas at Gondar, a haunting reminder of the pageantry of centuries gone by.

deserts, Ethiopia was influenced — but never quite dominated — by any of them.

By the first century AD Axum was the capital of a sizeable empire controlling the northern highlands and in constant touch with Egypt and Greece through her main port of Adulis (now lying buried in Eritrea some 40 kilometres south of the present-day port of Massawa).

Early in the 4th century a Syrian boy and his brother were taken to Axum after being stranded in Adulis. The boy, Frumentius, grew up in Axum and succeeded in converting the ruler of the time, King Ezana, to Christianity. When Frumentius went to Alexandria to inform the Patriarch that a bishop was required in Axum, the latter consecrated Frumentius as the bishop.

The early coins of Ezana's reign bear the crescent and the sun's disc — representing the moon and the sun that Axumites traditionally worshipped — while later coins bear the cross, the symbol of his new faith. Under King Kaleb (AD 514-542) much of the Arabian peninsula came under Christian rule and was subject to Axum. The Roman Emperor Justinian secured Kaleb's help in promoting trade in silk and spices from India to Europe through the Red Sea. By this time Ge'ez had replaced Sabaean as the court language of Axum.

The rise of Islam in the seventh century, however, drove the Axumites back across the Red Sea into their natural highland strongholds. By the eighth century Ethiopia was isolated from the outside world to such an extent that — as Gibbon put it so poetically — the Ethiopians "encompassed on all sides by the enemies of their religion, slept near a thousand years, forgetful of the world by whom they were forgotten".

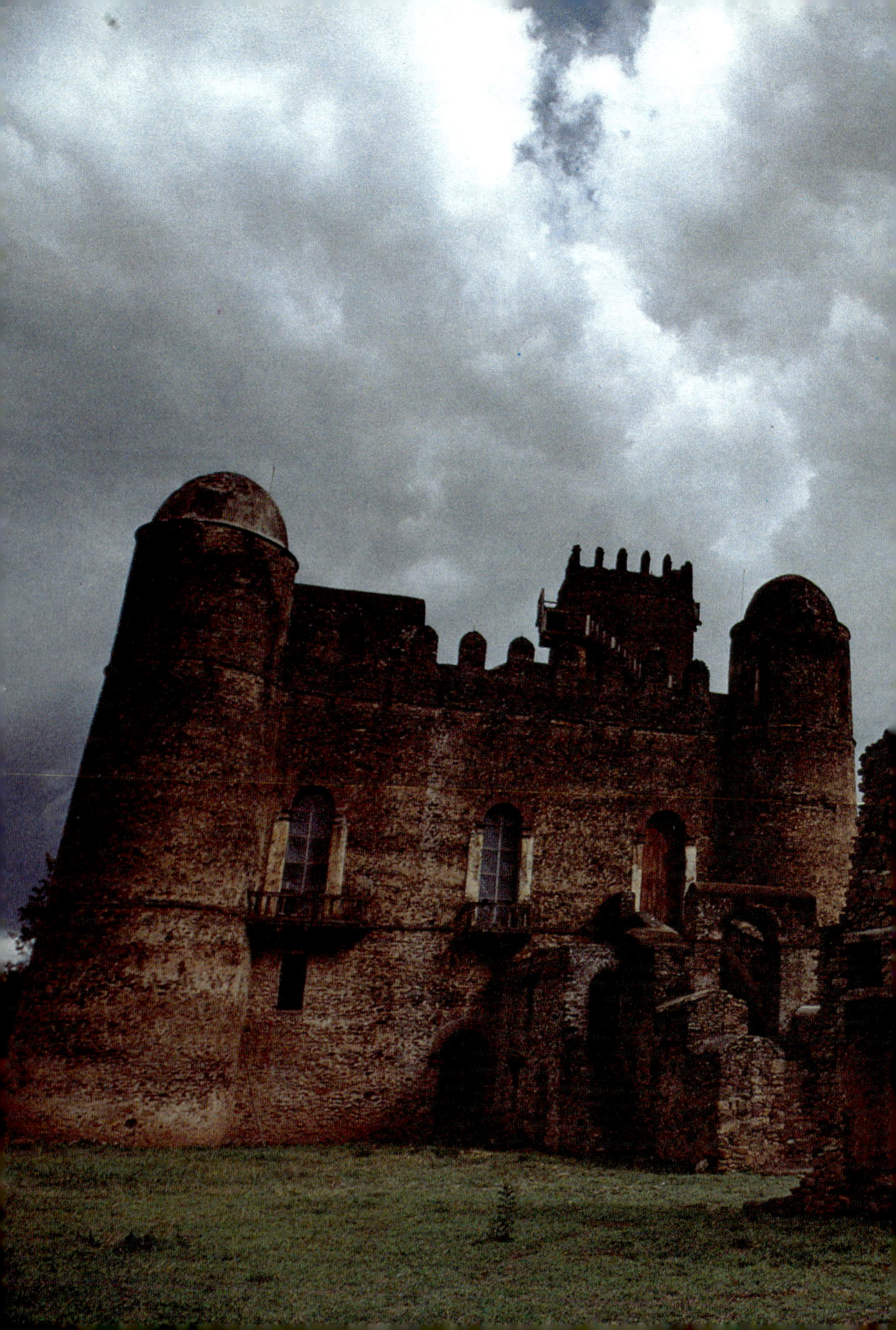

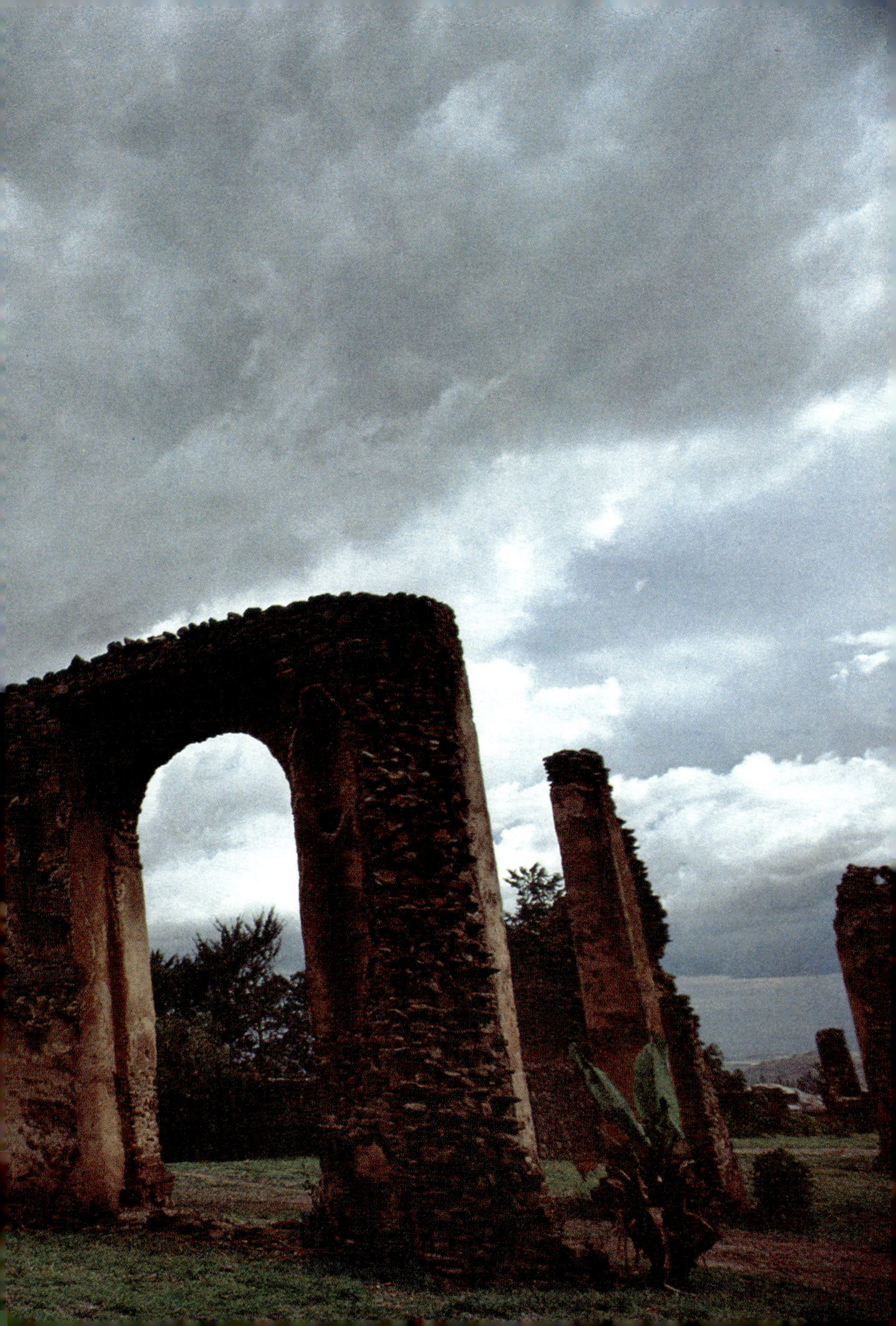

THE MIDDLE AGES

But on the highlands of Ethiopia those years were not wholly uneventful. With all foreign commercial and cultural contacts cut off, the country, still under central control from Axum, gradually extended its sphere of political and cultural influence southwards. Late in the 10th century the King of Axum was overthrown by the pagan Queen Judith (known as 'the monstrous one') who had his sons murdered. For nearly three hundred years thereafter Ethiopia was ruled by the new Zagwe dynasty established in their capital at Roha (now known as Lalibela) in Lasta.

The year 1270 witnessed the restoration of the Solomonic dynasty when Yekuno Amlak, who claimed descent from an Axumite prince who had fled south to escape Judith's wrath, ascended the throne. During the sub-sequent era the country was ruled by *Rases* (warlords) and *Shums* (chiefs) who would themselves submit to the king of their respective province or region and, through him, to the king of kings *(neguse negest).* Thus, the extensive domains, kingdoms and provinces of Ethiopia were ceaselessly subjected to mutually feuding temporal pressures and personalities.

In 1531 General Ahmed Ibn Ibrahim, nicknamed *Gragn* ('the left-handed'), entered the Ethiopian highlands at the head of a Muslim army that he had raised from Harar. Emperor Lebna Dengel (1508-1540) fled to Lake Tana and appealed to Portugal for military assistance. It was following this appeal that Christopher da Gama, son of the famous explorer Vasco da Gama, arrived at Massawa with 400 men. He was killed, but his men joined the new Emperor Claudius and slew General Ahmed ibn Ibrahim near Lake Tana. Subsequently, in 1557, the Pope sent a Jesuit mission to Ethiopia in an attempt to convert

Overleaf: A mural depicting Saint George slaying the dragon, which adorns the walls of St Mary's church at Axum.

the country to Roman Catholicism. The Jesuits made little headway and were eventually banished from Ethiopia in the middle of the 17th century.

MODERN HISTORY

In the 1840s both France and Britain entered into treaties with King Sahle Sellassie of Shoa. But it was with the accession to power of King Menilek II that Ethiopia was thrown into the maelstrom of modern politics during Europe's 'scramble for Africa'. By a fraudulent mis-representation of an article in the Treaty of Wuchale which Italy had concluded with Menilek, Italy laid claim to Ethiopia as her protectorate. Britain and France supported Italy's claims and the three proceeded to attempt to divide up eastern Africa into respective spheres of influence. This attempt failed in Ethiopia, however. At the decisive Battle of Adwa on 1 March 1896, Ethiopia scored a resounding victory over Italian colonial forces, thereby succeeding in asserting her age-old freedom and independence.

Ethiopia's independence was subsequently recognised not only by the defeated Italians but also by the other Great Powers of the time. Within the country a dynamic spirit of unity was fostered. Menilek founded Addis Ababa as a new and permanent capital in which he established the embryonic government ministries of a centralised, modern state. Schools and roads were built. Work on a railway line from Djibouti to Addis Ababa commenced in October 1897. The line reached Dire Dawa on 24 September 1902 and Addis Ababa itself in 1917. The story of the attempted Italian conquest of Ethiopia, cut short at Adwa in 1896, did not end there, however. In December 1934 Italian forces opened fire on Ethiopian troops at Walwal in the Ogaden. This incident was the precursor to

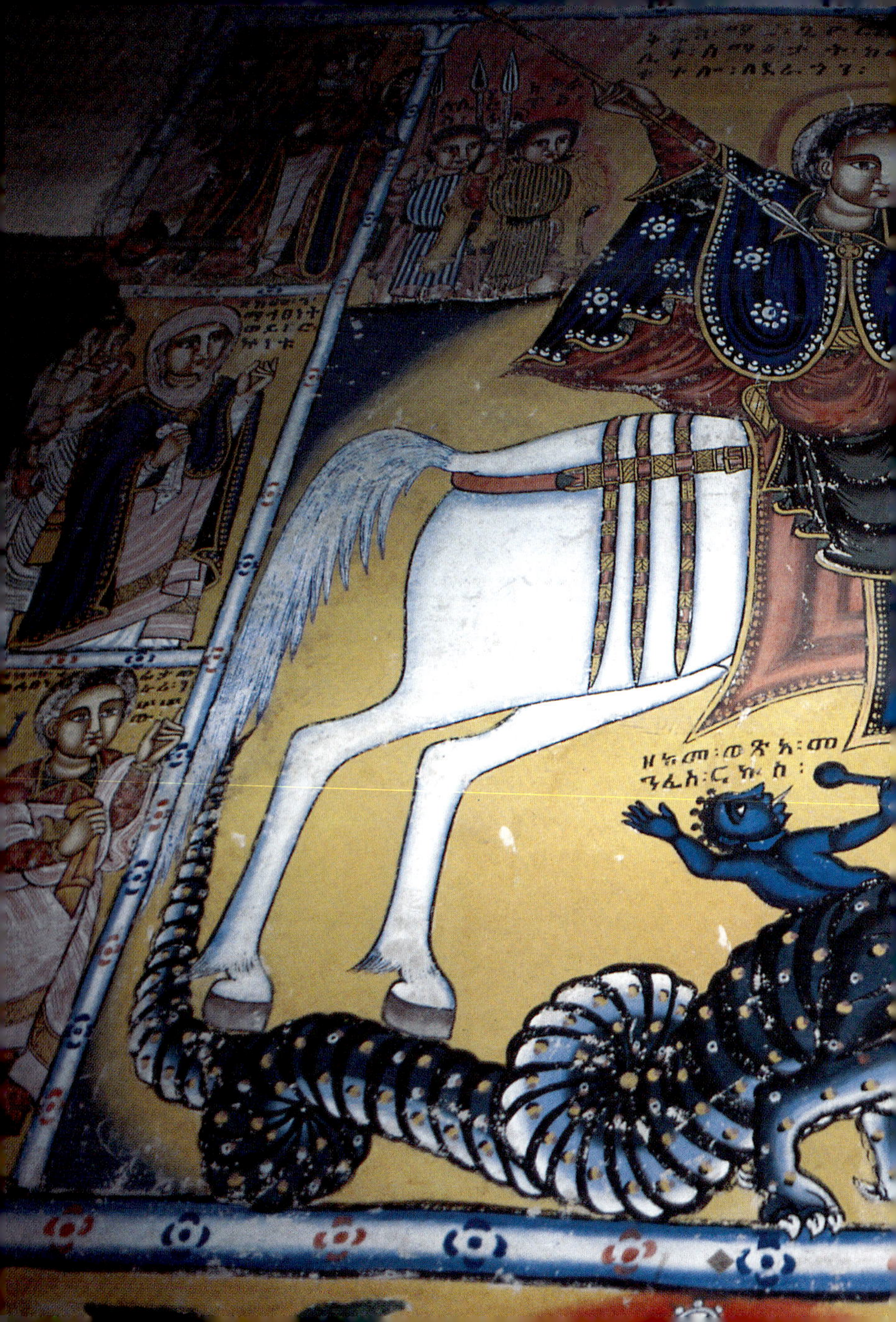
ዘኤመ፡ወጽአ፡መ
ንፈስ፡ርኩስ፡

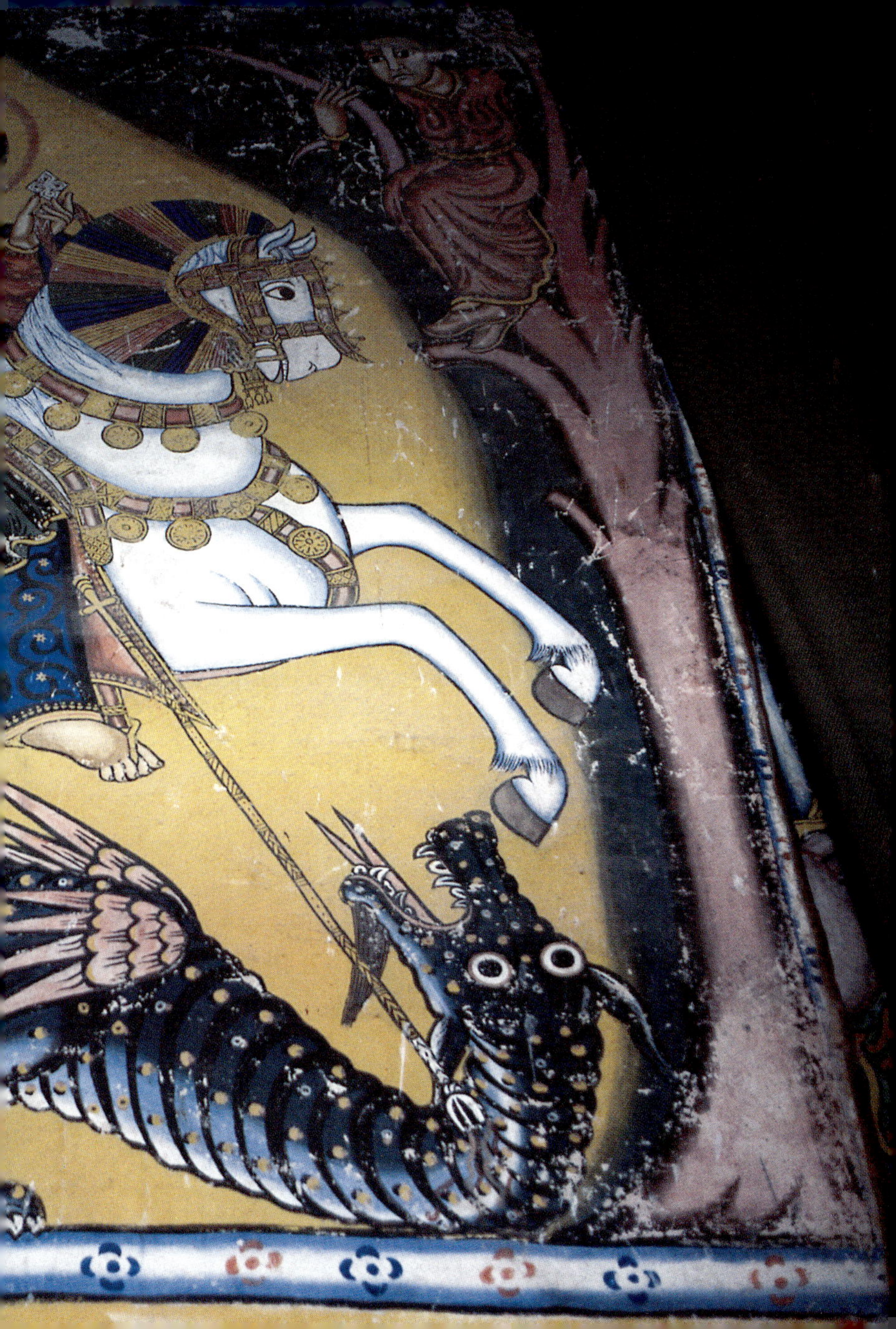

a devastating series of attacks, amounting to a full-scale — if undeclared — war and leading to the Italian occupation of Ethiopia from 1936 to 1941. Ethiopian patriots carried out guerilla warfare throughout the five years of occupation and were, after the outbreak of World War II, finally joined by the Allied forces who helped them to regain their lost independence.

However, unrest continued in the north. After 11 years of British administration, Eritrea was federated with Ethiopia in 1952. In 1962 the federation was abolished and Eritrea was integrated into Ethiopia as one of her 15 administrative regions.

In September 1974 Selassie was toppled by military council — the Derg — and eventually Mariam Haile Mengistu, one of the officers, became head of state and Ethiopia fell into a state of civil war. Mengistu fled into exile in 1991 just before the fall of Addis Ababa. After years of conflict, the new provisional government set about reshaping the country. One of the first outcomes of the new system was to grant Eritrea independence as a nation in its own right.

Chapter 3 · Arts and Crafts

Ethiopia shares with Egypt the visible remains of a rich, ancient culture. But whereas Egypt's golden age was most closely associated with the Pharaohs, Ethiopia's arts sprang from her early Christian heritage. In a land of 15,000 churches, religious art has permeated much of the culture and priests share with warriors a love of richly embroidered and colourful costumes. Places of worship are often living museums of exquisite vestments.

Ethiopia possesses an ancient civilisation, over 80 language groups, a unique alphabet, a varied geography, and a strategic location at the crossroads of Asia, Europe and Africa. These are some of the factors that have endowed the country with a truly eclectic but distinctly rich tradition of arts and crafts ranging from prehistoric cave paintings and tools to contemporary art forms.

Yared, the sixth-century Ethiopian saint to whom is attributed the creation of the formalised sacred music and dance unique to this country was the first man to devise and use an original system of musical notation in Africa. The system has three modes, or moods, and a complex notation of 700 signs.

ORNAMENT

The Ethiopian love of ornament, design and aesthetic art is reflected not only in the dress of the people but also in their personal adornment and domestic utensils. The country is a treasure-house of jewellery.

Especially so are the monasteries and churches with their jewel-studded crowns and diadems, and with their daggers and shields set with rubies and emeralds. Jewellery and ornament form an important part of Ethiopian dress, thus keeping alive the traditional craftsmanship of goldsmiths and silversmiths.

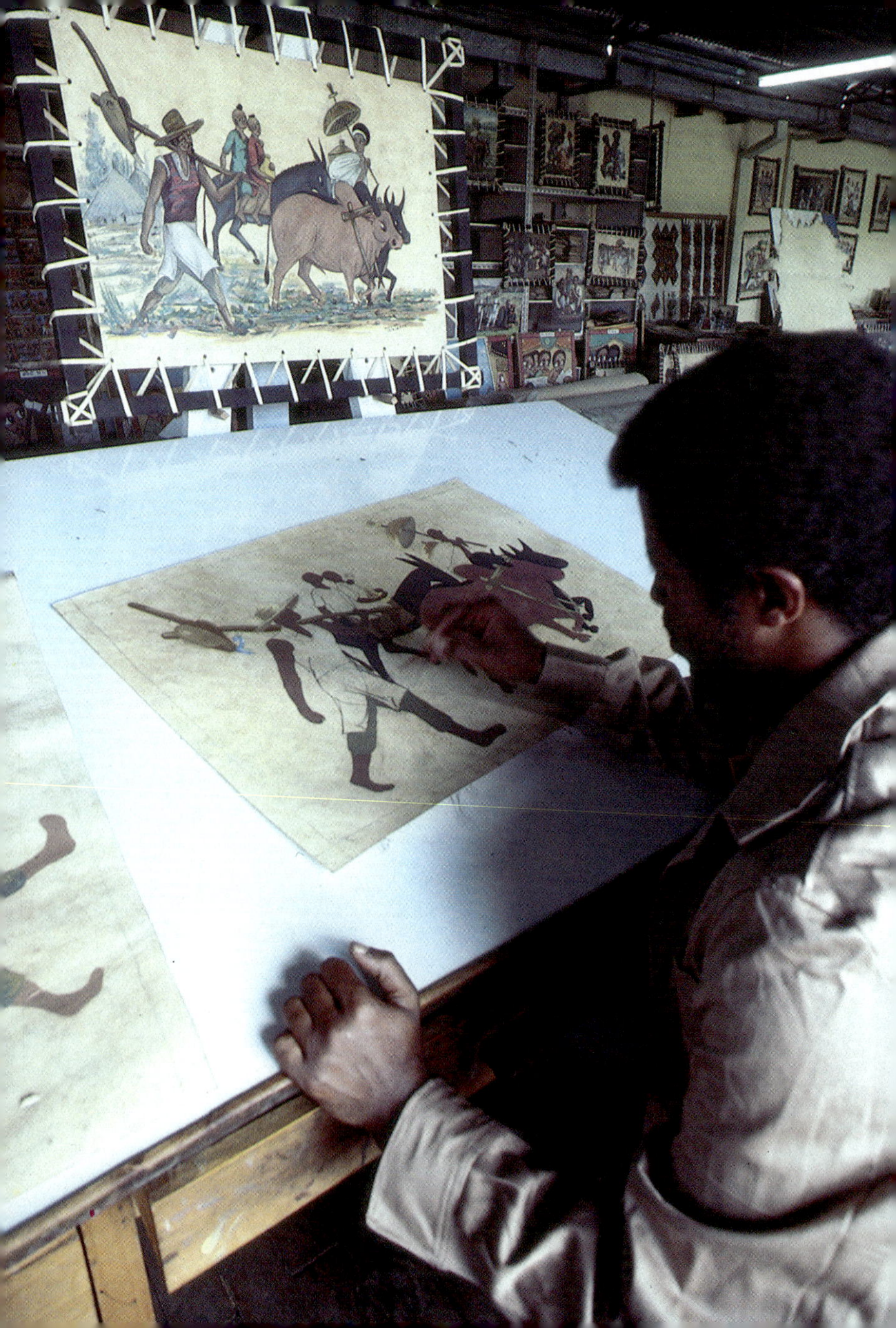

Opposite: An artisan painting on parchment.

Below: A modern stained-glass mural-window at Africa Hall, by Master-Artist Afework Tekle.

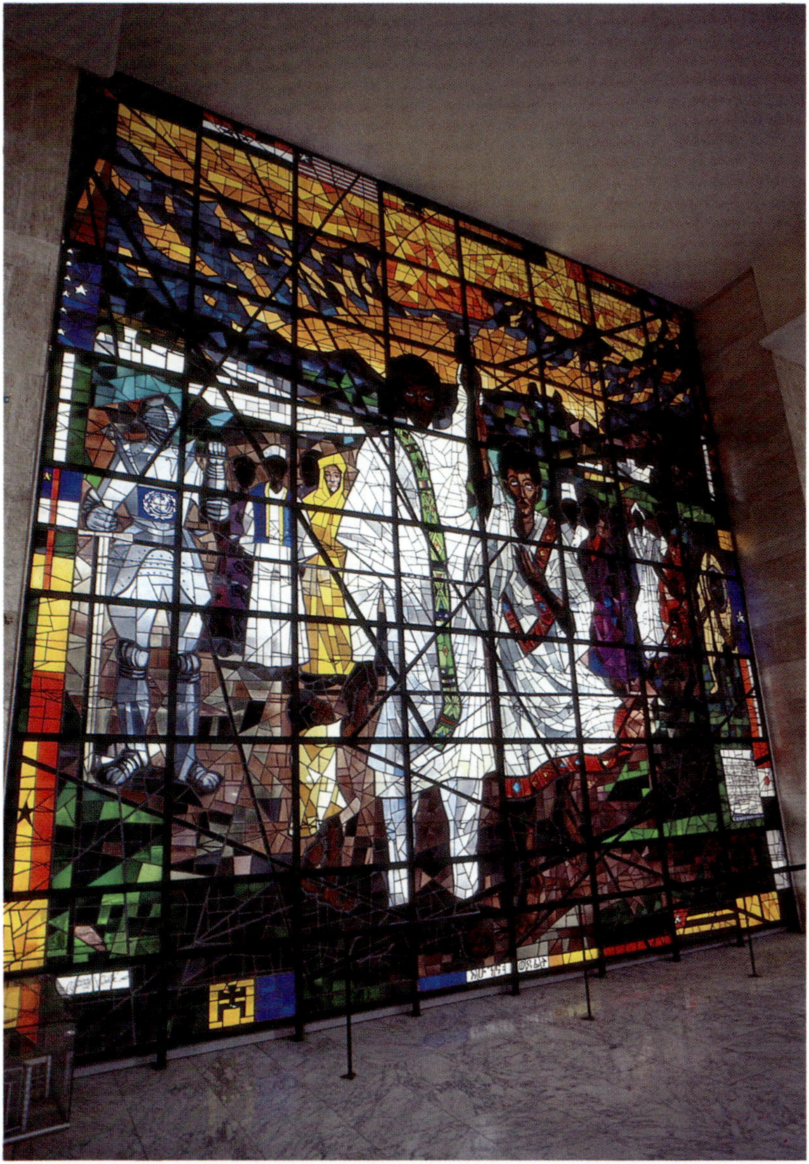

The same creative tradition is maintained also by the humbler — but no less impressive — skills of the rural weavers of grass, leather and hair; stringers of colourful glass-bead necklaces and cowrie shells; decorators of gourds; and tattooers of the human body.

PARCHMENT PAINTINGS

The monasteries of Ethiopia produced some of the earliest illuminated parchments. These are of high standard in book decoration and have contributed a great deal to establishing a traditional style of painting on parchment. Priceless Ethiopian manuscripts can be found in libraries and museums in Leningrad, Leipzig, Vienna, the Vatican, London and elsewhere. The Bibliotheque Nationale in Paris possesses no fewer than 1,000 of these ancient manuscripts. Good, modern examples of brightly coloured illustrated stories drawn from Ethiopian history and the Bible are produced in large quantities, and despite the repetitiveness of subject matter individual artists produce very distinctive parchment paintings. The popular story revolving around the visit of the Queen of Sheba to the Court of King Solomon has given us perhaps the oldest comic strip in history.

The ancient tradition of religious art is still very much alive. However younger artists, many of them exceptionally gifted, have also evolved their own unique styles based on modern values, and this trend is particularly evident over the last 30 years.

MURALS

Church decorations, which in Ethiopia are second only to manuscript illumination in importance, are another medium for artistic expression. Many Ethiopian masterpieces may never be known to the outside world because they are painted on the walls and ceilings of remote and inaccessible churches or monasteries. A prodigious quantity of such murals exists, as well as small wooden panels, or triptychs, adorning the interior of practically every church — both old and new — in Ethiopia.

MUSICAL INSTRUMENTS

Ethiopia's music and dances have their own distinctive characteristics and are tremendously varied in style and content.

Like many other elements of Ethiopian culture, the country's music has affinities with both African and Levantine forms of artistic expression. In Ethiopia, the north African arabesque chromatic style meets and comes to terms with the more simple pentatonic musical world of central Africa. This merging of instruments and styles from various sources has led to the development of musical traditions that are unique to this mountainous country. Among the most commonly-used instruments are a wide variety of drums similar to those found elsewhere on the continent. Side by side with these, however, are instruments unique to Ethiopia, such as the six-stringed *krar* believed to have originated from the 'kinnor' or the Hebrew Lyre. Similarly, the *begena,* the largest and most dignified of Ethiopian string instruments, which resembles the Lyre of the Greeks and Romans, is believed to be a replica of the biblical harp of David. The most popular traditional instrument is the *masenko,* a diamond-shaped one-stringed horse-hair fiddle and the only Ethiopian instrument played with a bow. Some of the wind instruments, made of bamboo

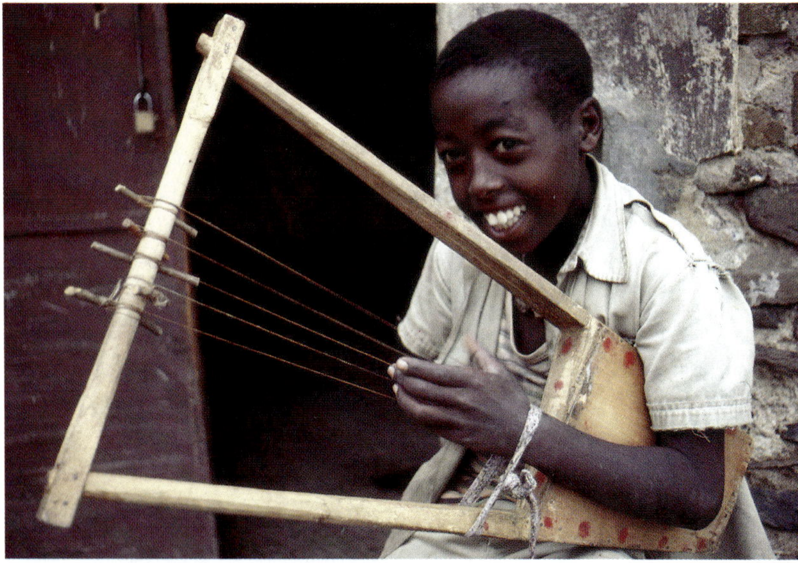

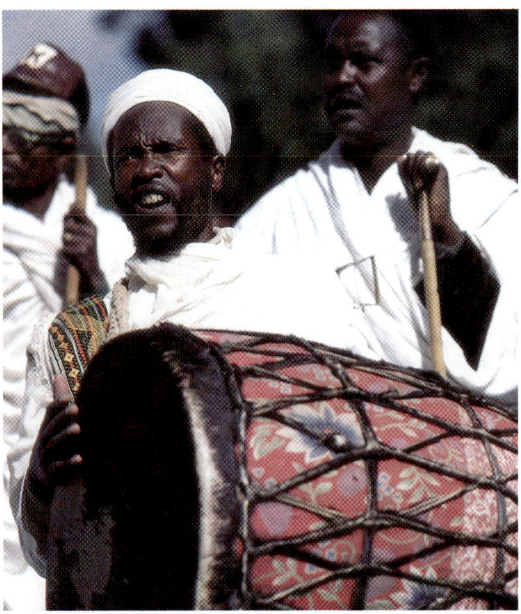

Above: Young minstrel playing the krar.

Left: All church music is accompanied by sistrums, hand-bells and drums such as this kebero.

Opposite: The mural shows St Yared, the founder of Ethiopia's liturgical music, playing the sistrum for his king. Both men are so entranced that when the ruler drops his spear, piercing the musician's foot, neither man notices.

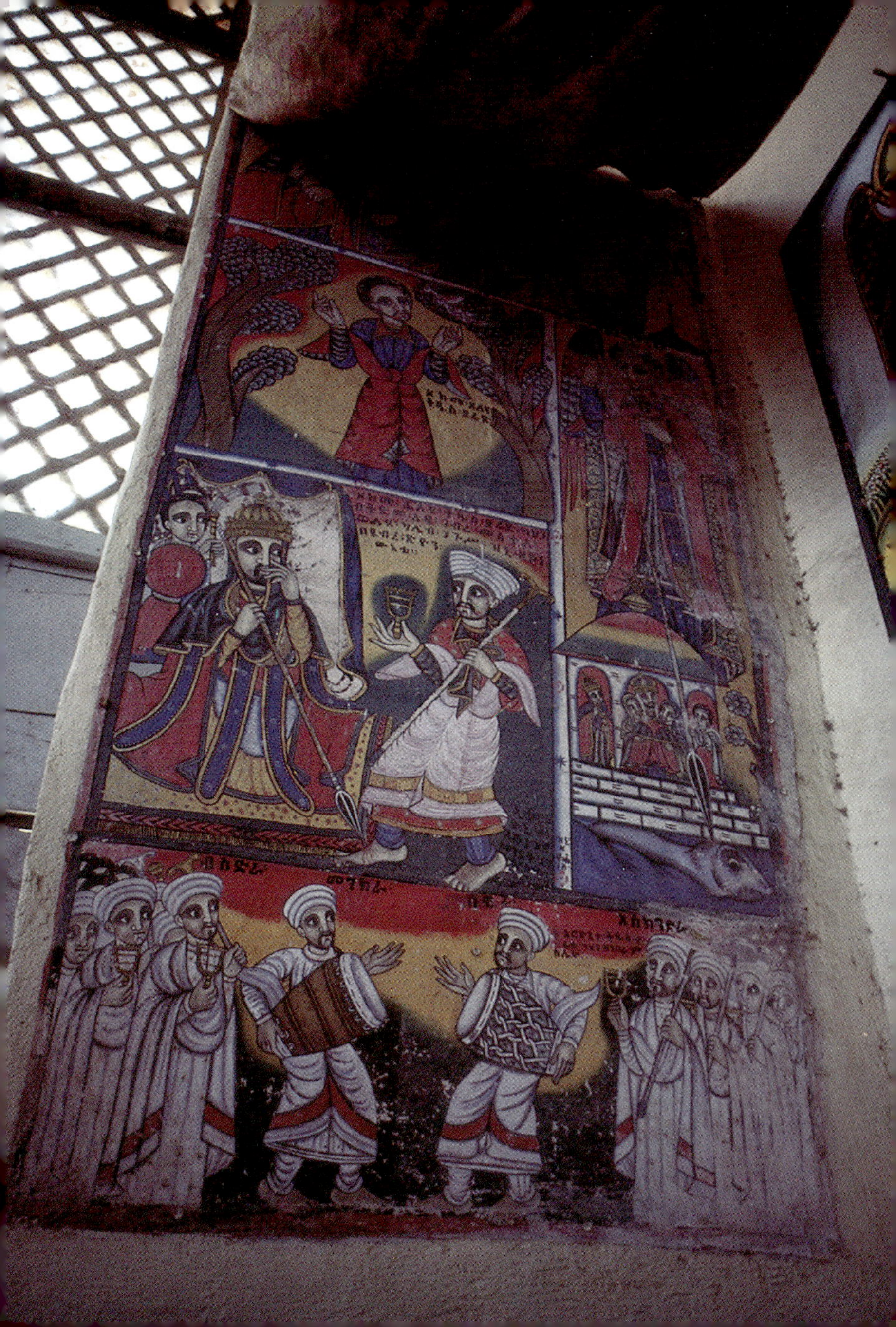

cane, are the *washint* popular with shepherds, and the *embilta*, a ceremonial instrument devoid of finger-holes, used for heralding. The *meleket* is another wind instrument; resembling a trumpet, it is about a metre in length, has a bugle-type cap and no finger-holes. The longest bamboo instruments are the *chechazey* (made from bamboo enclosed in a cow's oesophagus). The extraordinary *dinkey* is 4.5 to 6 metres in length.

The *negarit* is a small kettle-drum of about 45 centimetres in diameter. The *kebero*, another type of kettle-drum, comes in a wide variety of sizes and shapes, though it is usually tall and slender. The *atamo* is a small drum held in the hand, under the arm or between the knees of the player. The kebero, *tsinatsil* (sistrum), and the *qatchel*, a small hand-bell, are all used in church ceremonies.

CHURCH MUSIC AND DANCE

Ethiopian ecclesiastical music merits the term classical. It is quite different from the folk music of the country and its mastery requires years of rigorous training. Its origin and development are something of a mystery, although it is believed that some of its elaborate and exotic dances may have come down from the mystery cults of ancient Egypt. Saint Yared, as noted above, is said to have composed the entire body of liturgical music. If this is indeed the case then he achieved a great deal. Music and dance within the Ethiopian Orthodox Church are not — like the hymns and chants of other churches — just additions to Mass or prayer; they constitute integral parts of the religious ceremony. And while they remain formal and solemn, the singing and the movements of the *debteras* (the church scholar-musicians) make for a lively, dramatic and mystifying show. As Edward Ullendorf states, "the entire spectacle, the carriage of the *Tabot* (Ark of the Covenant) in solemn procession, accompanied by singing, dancing, beating of staffs or prayer sticks, rattling of sistrum and the sounding of drums, has caused all who have witnessed it to feel transported".

FOLK DANCE

Religious festivals, along with secular feasts and weddings, provide ideal occasions for folk dance in Ethiopia. A great deal of the colour in the *Timket* (Epiphany) and *Meskal* (the Finding of the True Cross) comes from the dancing done by the huge crowd of people gathered to observe the occasion. After the ceremony proper, the crowd breaks up into smaller groups to sing and dance for much of the day. In Ethiopia singing seldom takes place without some dancing, although there is variation as to what part of the song is accompanied by dance.

There are all kinds of folk dances employing all forms and combinations of stamping, jumping, skipping, shaking, turning and twisting. Minjar has perhaps the most eclectic dance utilising shoulders, footwork, skipping, square-dance movements and dance-drama. With the Gurage, footwork is the most important part of the dance. By contrast, the Wolaita from southern Ethiopia employ more intricate legwork and a more total participation of the whole body, set against the rhythm of drums. The Wolaita can provoke raucous laughter just by dancing with a stick. The Dorze have a form of dance which emphasises acrobatic skills; somersaults and cartwheels abound. With the Kotu (a branch of the Oromos living in Harerge) it is the head that does most of the movement.

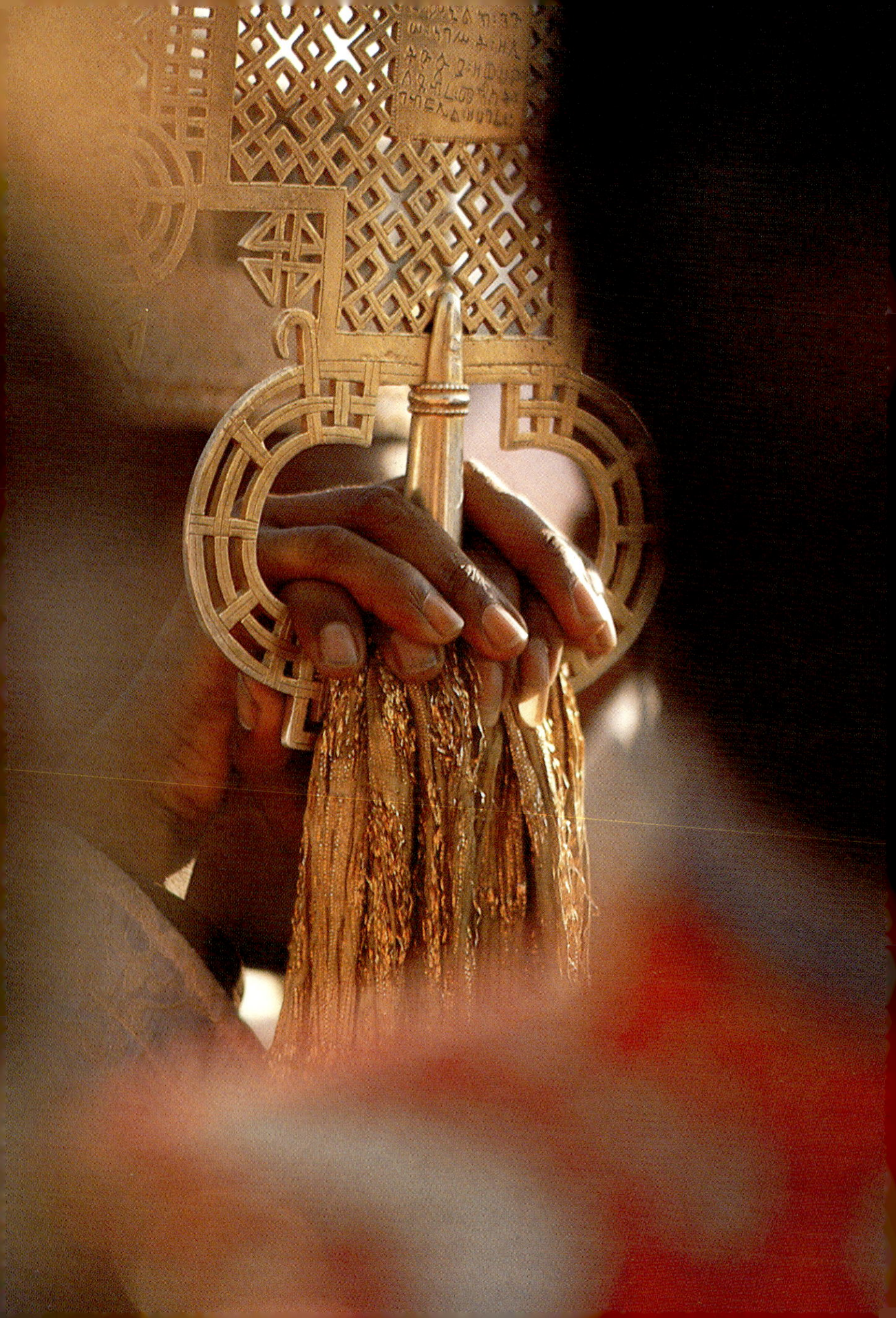

Left: An Axumite cross. The cloth is used when holding the cross, to keep it clean.

Below: The 'dove's wings' indicate that this cross was made in Lalibela.

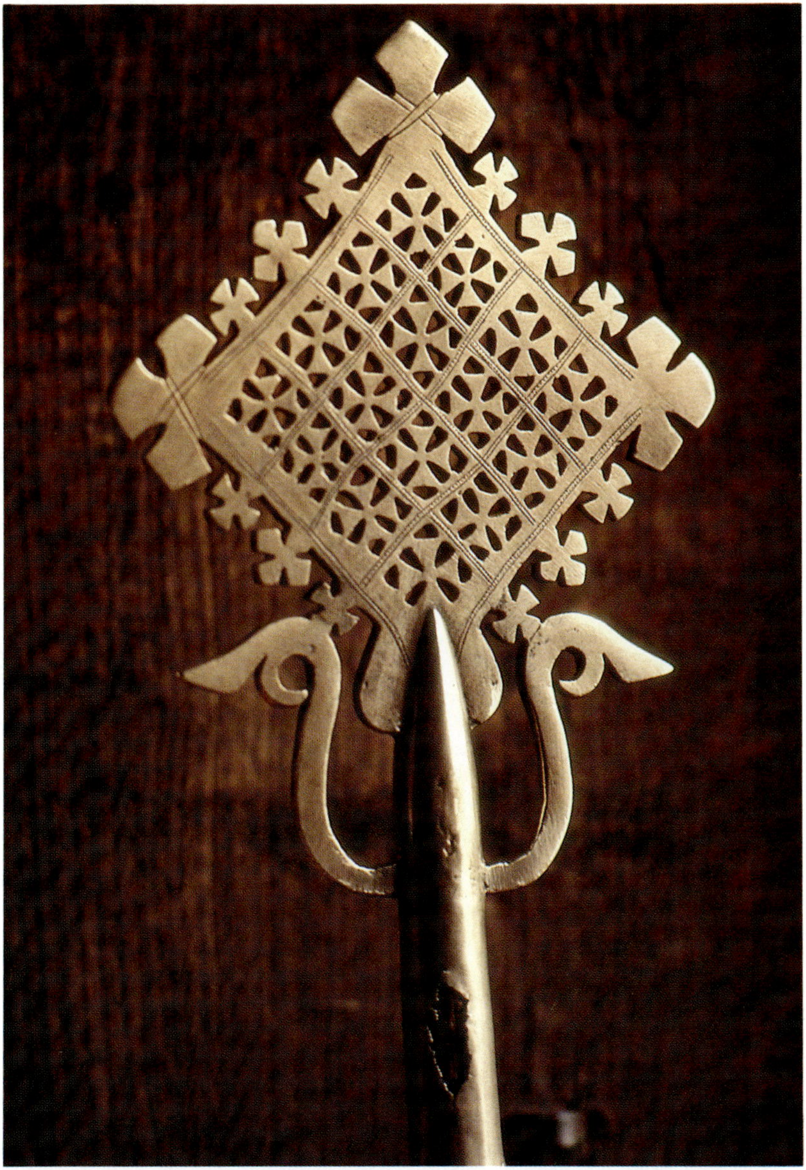

Despite all this diversity there are certain characteristics of Ethiopian folk dance which are general and widespread — at least amongst highlanders. One of the main types of dance movements in Ethiopia, the *eskista*, or shoulder dance, is, for all practical purposes, common to most of them. In *eskista* the shoulders and chest move, rather than the feet. However, several techniques are employed — jerking, shaking or twisting — and the direction of the shoulder movements can be horizontal, vertical or diagonal. With women the movement of the breasts is also significant. These subtle differences allow the eskista to express a whole range of emotions — from the softest feeling of love, through the ecstasy of happiness to the wildest explosion of warlike spirit. These movements reveal the very soul and the different moods of the revelling Ethiopians.

Although intricate footwork rarely accompanies eskista, this does not mean that the dancers stand still. On the contrary, they walk, turn, jump and sometimes crouch almost to the ground. At moments of almost manic excitement the dancers draw air sharply through the teeth, making a susurration sounding like 'eskista'.

Another popular song-dance in Ethiopia — a war dance — is the *fukera*, performed by warriors, their heads adorned by lions' manes, and carrying spears and shields. Between verses in which the warrior recounts his exploits he dances, holding his spear horizontally across his shoulders, moving his head from left to right, with his face set in a ferocious expression.

POTTERY

The potter's craft in Ethiopia goes back to the pre-Axumite civilisation of around 1,000 BC. The traditional potter, usually a woman, used only a knife-shaped bone and a piece of goat skin for moulding her pots into shape; the design being plain, with simple, incised geometric patterns. Superb traditional pottery is today produced by monks at the Sambo Tree Monastery in the north-east of the country. Monks prepare the clay while the nuns mould pots into shape. Gurage pots are embossed with knobs in a peculiar fashion and have loops for hanging them up when not in use.

The Falashas of Gondar (followers of Judaism), traditional potters and blacksmiths, are unique in that they alone fashion human and animal figurines in stylised form.

CARVING

Carving is another traditional craft which continues to flourish in some parts of the country. Kaffa, with its hardy timber, produces some of the finest wood-carving in the country. The very popular three-legged Jimma stool is carved from the solid trunk of the *shola* (sycamore) tree. Other carved objects made of wood include combs (of which the most ornate are used by the Afar people), rosary beads, bowls, camel bells, coffee urns, butter pots, and headrests. Covers for the Bible and prayer books are also carved from wood.

Chairs, tables, stools, portable altars and, in some of the churches, remarkable ceilings, some dating back to early Christian times, bear intricately carved and beautiful designs.

HORNWORK

The horns of oxen, buffalo, ibex and oryx are made into various decorative and utilitarian objects. Drinking mugs are the most usual, but horn is also used for walking sticks, light fittings and jewellery.

Below: A processional cross in the Axumite style.

Opposite: Priest of Lalibela holding a wooden cross.

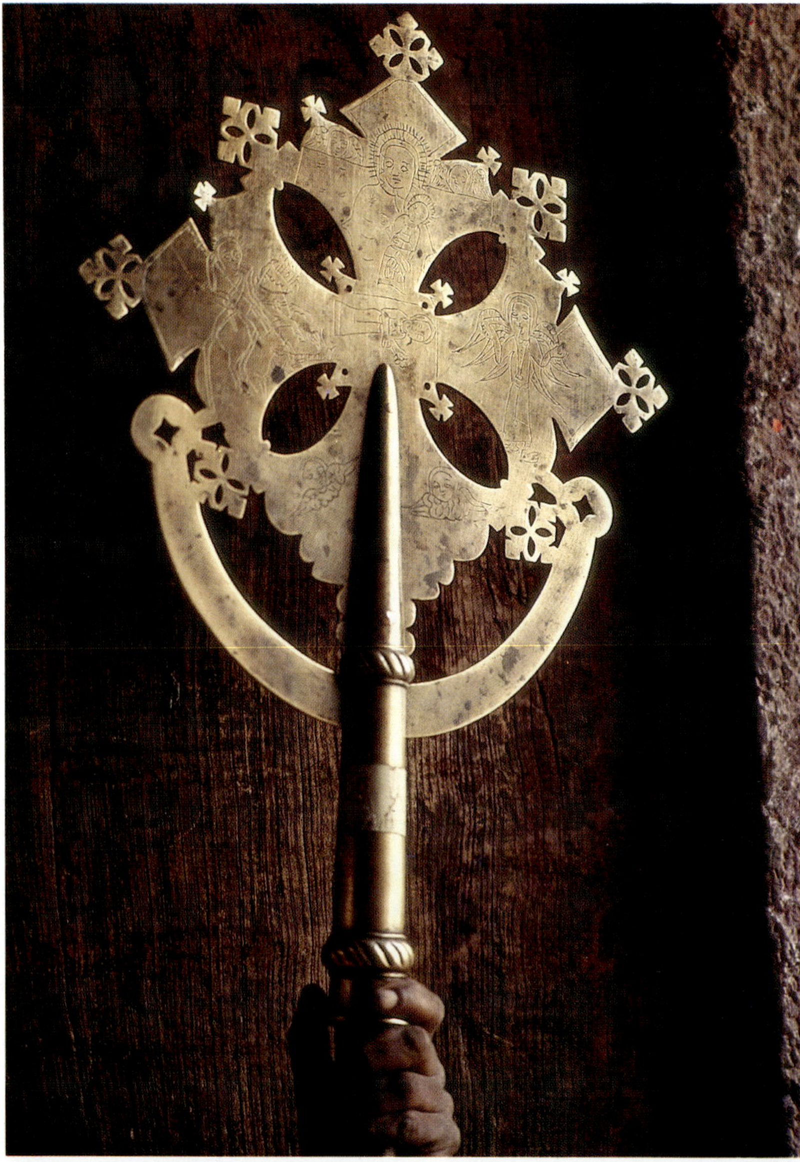

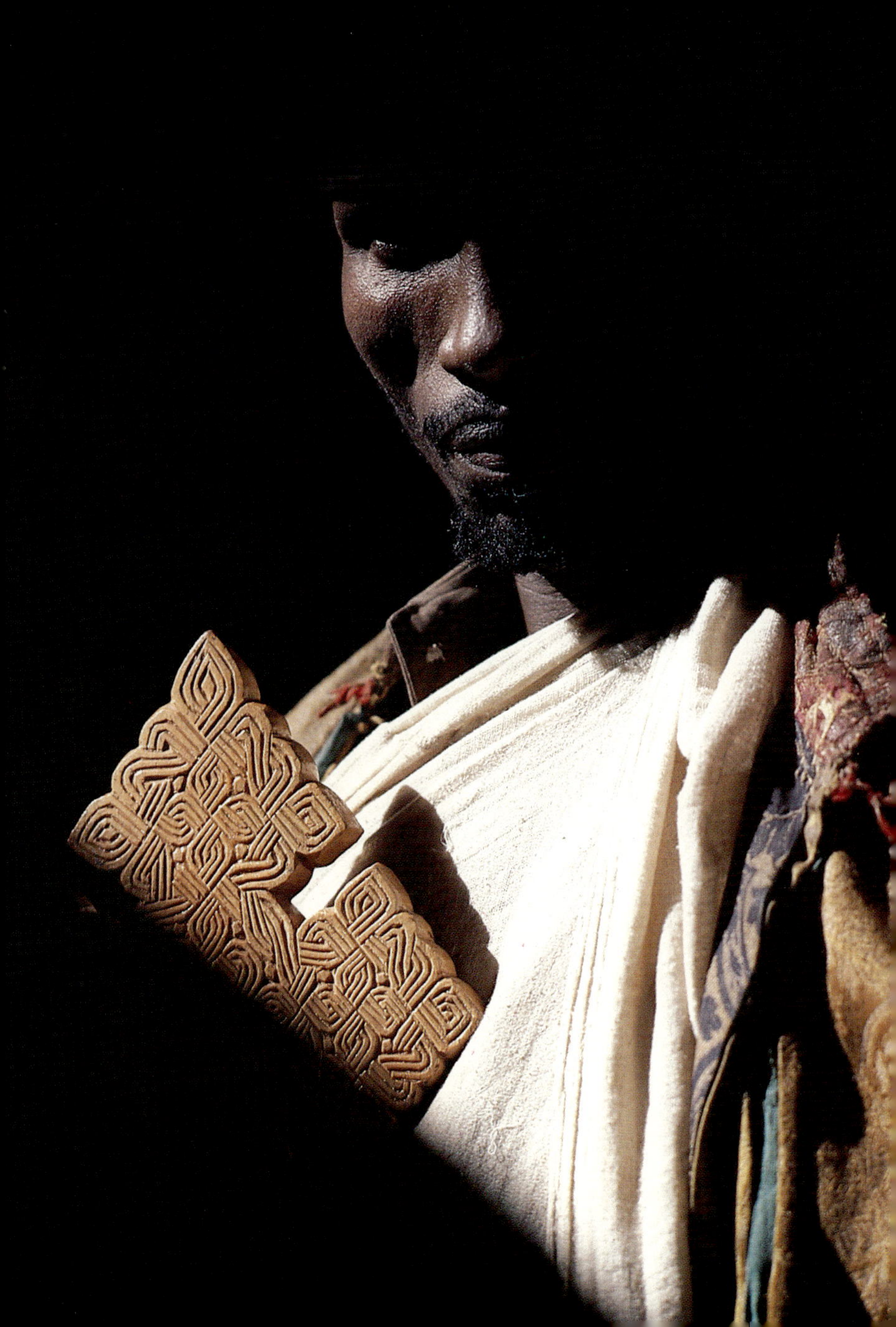

WEAPONRY

Shields traditionally used by noblemen were made of skins, sometimes covered with velvet, and richly ornamented with metal embossing or filigree work. Shields for warriors were made of rhinoceros or hippopotamus hides and ornamented with raised bumps. Other accoutrements of Ethiopian warriors included finely made daggers, swords and spears, with richly designed scabbards of metal or leather.

WICKERWORK

Basket weaving is perhaps one of the most highly developed of all the crafts. The basket weavers of Harar are particularly famous. Woven from different coloured grasses and fibres, their wares are highly prized for their intricate designs. The *mesob,* a brightly fashioned tray woven into a conical basket, used as a table — or with its lid on, as a food container — is exclusive to Ethiopia.

CROSSES AND METALWORK

Oral tradition has it that after the conflict between Islam and Christianity began, an Ethiopian emperor issued an edict commanding all his subjects to wear a cross around the neck to prove fidelity to their faith. Perhaps because of this hundreds of thousands of crosses of gold, silver, brass and other metals are to be found in Ethiopia. They range from small pendants made of delicate gold and silver filigree, or wrought in silver, gold, and iron, to huge processional crosses, and to the smaller hand crosses with characteristic square bases carried by priests. The symbolism, shape and style of other forms of Ethiopian metalwork vary according to the region or period of making. From *couk mawchas* (earwax cleaners) to incense burners, from the old silver filigree of Harar and Keren to the gilded and glittering crowns of Axum, they are highly refined works of art that are the result of a long indigenous tradition.

LEATHERWORK

Ethiopia has the largest livestock population in Africa — and one of the largest in the world in terms of per capita distribution. Because of this animal products in general have an important place in the life of Ethiopians — and perhaps none more so than leather.

There are leather mats, leather skirts, leather hats, leather cloaks and coveralls, leather sacks, leather milk pots and butter containers, and even leather homes. Leather is also used in combination with straw, bamboo wood, beads and cowrie shells — as in, for example, the gorgeous milk and butter pots of Bale, the leather skirts of the Bena in Gamo Gofa, and the commonly seen *ankelba,* a baby-carrier strapped round the back of the mother. The traditional lunchbox is the *agelgil,* a leather-covered basket indigenous to Ethiopia, used also for carrying the personal effects of the bride to her new home. In addition there is a whole range of Ethiopian harnesses and riding equipment characterised by bright and blazing colours not usually associated with leather.

BEADS AND COWRIE SHELLS

Beads and cowrie shells are used as status symbols by some Ethiopian lowlanders. The Galeb and the Bume peoples of the Omo Valley adorn themselves with huge quantities of beads and also use beads to decorate household goods and clothing. The kaleidoscope of costumes, objects made from beads and

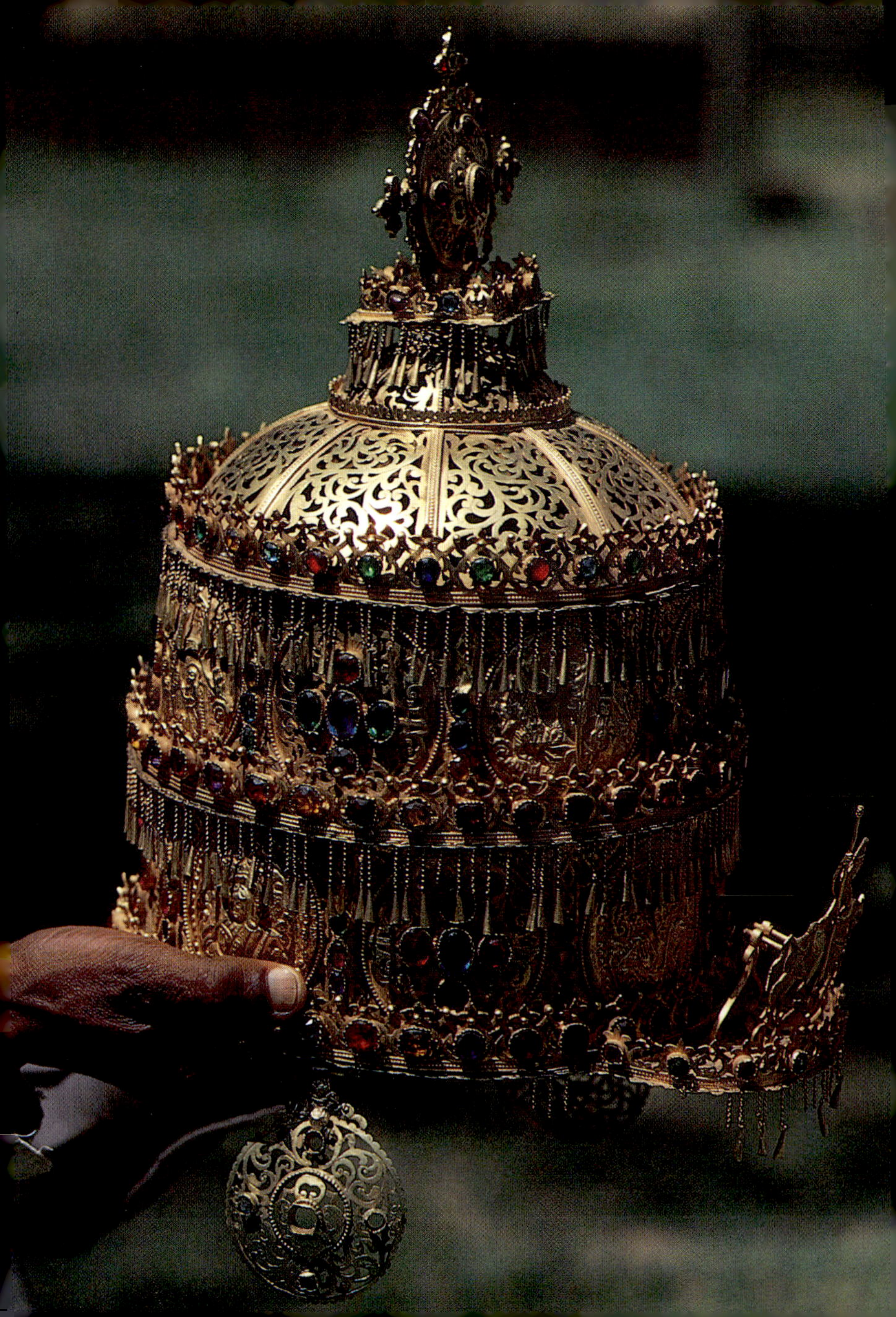

Opposite: Gold crown of Emperor Menilek II.

Below: Guji girl with decorated gourd.

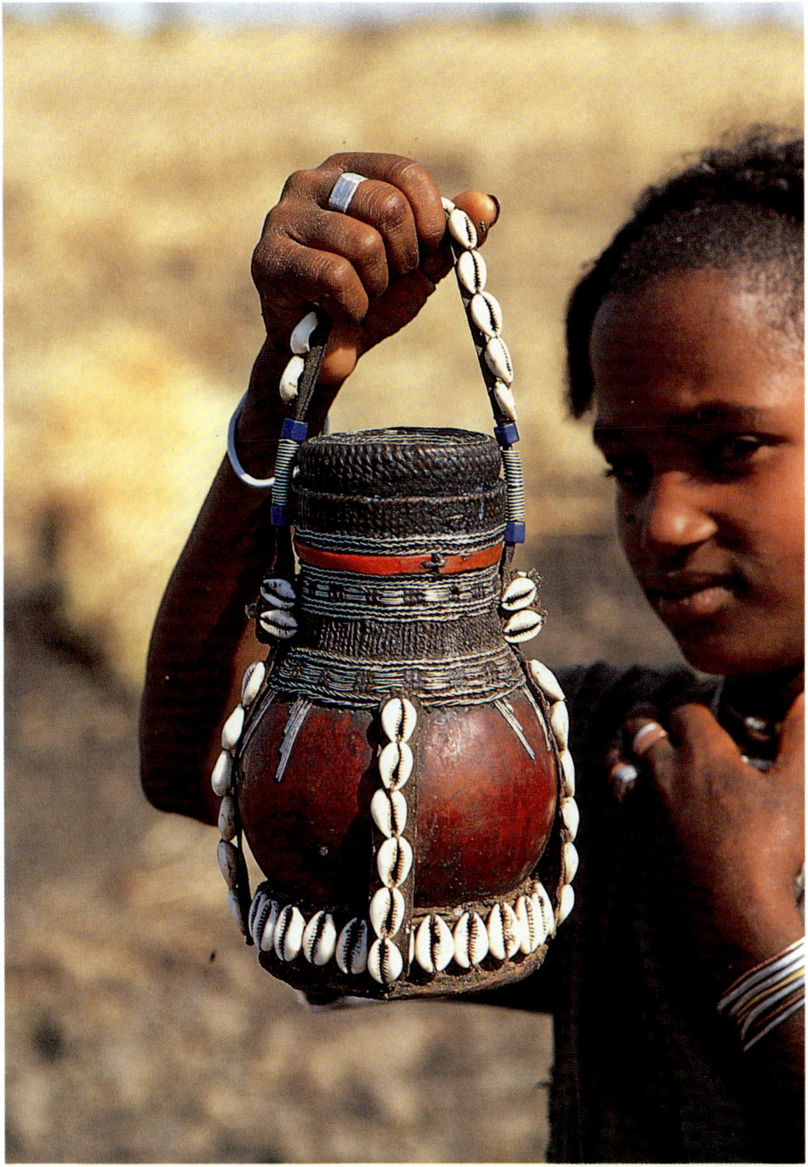

cowrie shells, and the great variety of decorative jewellery and coiffure found throughout Ethiopia are extensively documented in *Ethiopian Costumes*, a publication of the Ethiopian Tourism Commission.

WEAVING

As one approaches the village of Geech, high up in the Simien Mountains one sees small huts or sheds adjacent to the bigger dwellings. In these sheds are men standing in waist-high holes with their hands moving in front of them. The sight is curious and little does one suspect that the men are working with the simplest hand-and-foot looms. A similar method of weaving is employed by the Dorze of southern and central Ethiopia.

The Konso in Gamo Gofa, famous for their unique form of terraced agriculture, are also known for making huge cotton blankets called *boolooko*. It is common to see very old men sitting outside in the yard with a wad of fluffy cotton in one hand and an *inzirt* (the simple Ethiopian hand-threader, or distaff) in the other.

From simple wares like this to the intricate embroidery of the Dorze weaving has a rich and colourful history in Ethiopia. Fashion-conscious urban populations have given added impetus to the work of Ethiopian weavers and inspired the profusion of designs and patterns found today on the borders of *shammas* (shawls) and dresses.

The classical Ethiopian lion woven out of tan, black, brown and white woollen fibres has achieved international recognition, as have the finely patterned rugs made by the students of the Handicrafts School and the Ethio-Craft Rehabilitation Centre.

Overleaf: Lake Abyata, where thousands of flamingos and Great White pelicans come to feed.

A RENAISSANCE OF ETHIOPIAN FOLK CULTURE

Ethiopia's artists, craftsmen, and their trade have not always been accorded their due recognition. *Azmaris* (minstrels) and their profession were often belittled by the very people who enjoyed the sweet melodies of their *masenko* (a one-stringed musical instrument). Likewise, weavers, potters, smiths and scribes were not duly respected. Folk culture and with it folk song and dance, were neglected — and not appreciated — outside their restricted localities.

All this is changing. Today artists and craftsmen practise their trade with pride as they make their own contribution to cultural and social development in Ethiopia. Every town, and in most cases every *kebele* (neighbourhood association) has its own *kinet guad* (cultural troupe) and its own cultural hall. A *kinet guad* is made up of amateur singers, dancers, poets and writers, working with the song, dance and folklore of the nation; each troupe specialises in re-creating the folk culture, dance and music of its particular area. The repertoire of the professional national troupe is, however, a medley of all of Ethiopia's different cultures. These troupes put on entertaining skits, dance-dramas and musical shows on special occasions.

With regard to the crafts, every kind of assistance and encouragement is given to all craftsmen. Organising, modernising and developing cottage industries is now a national concern.

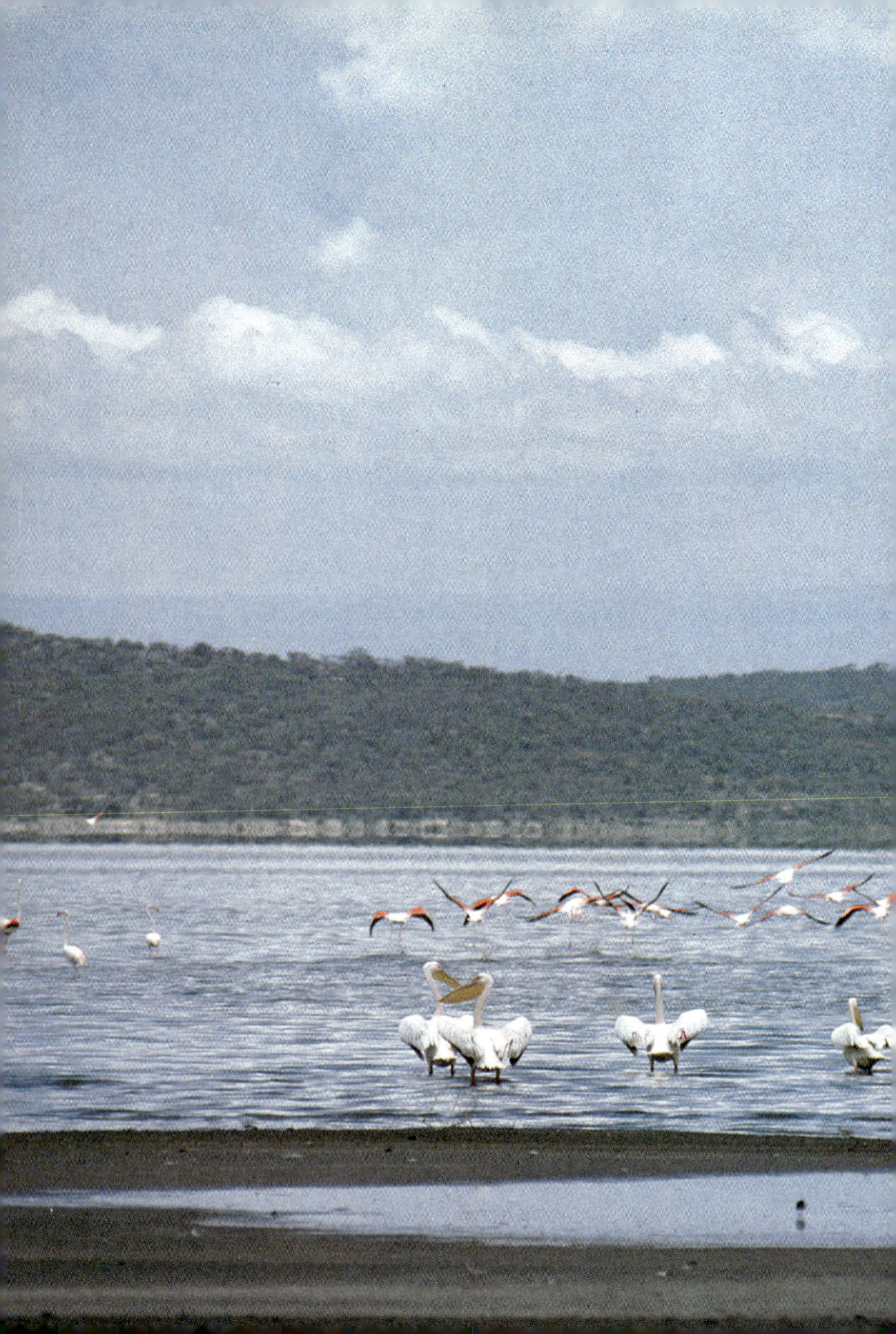

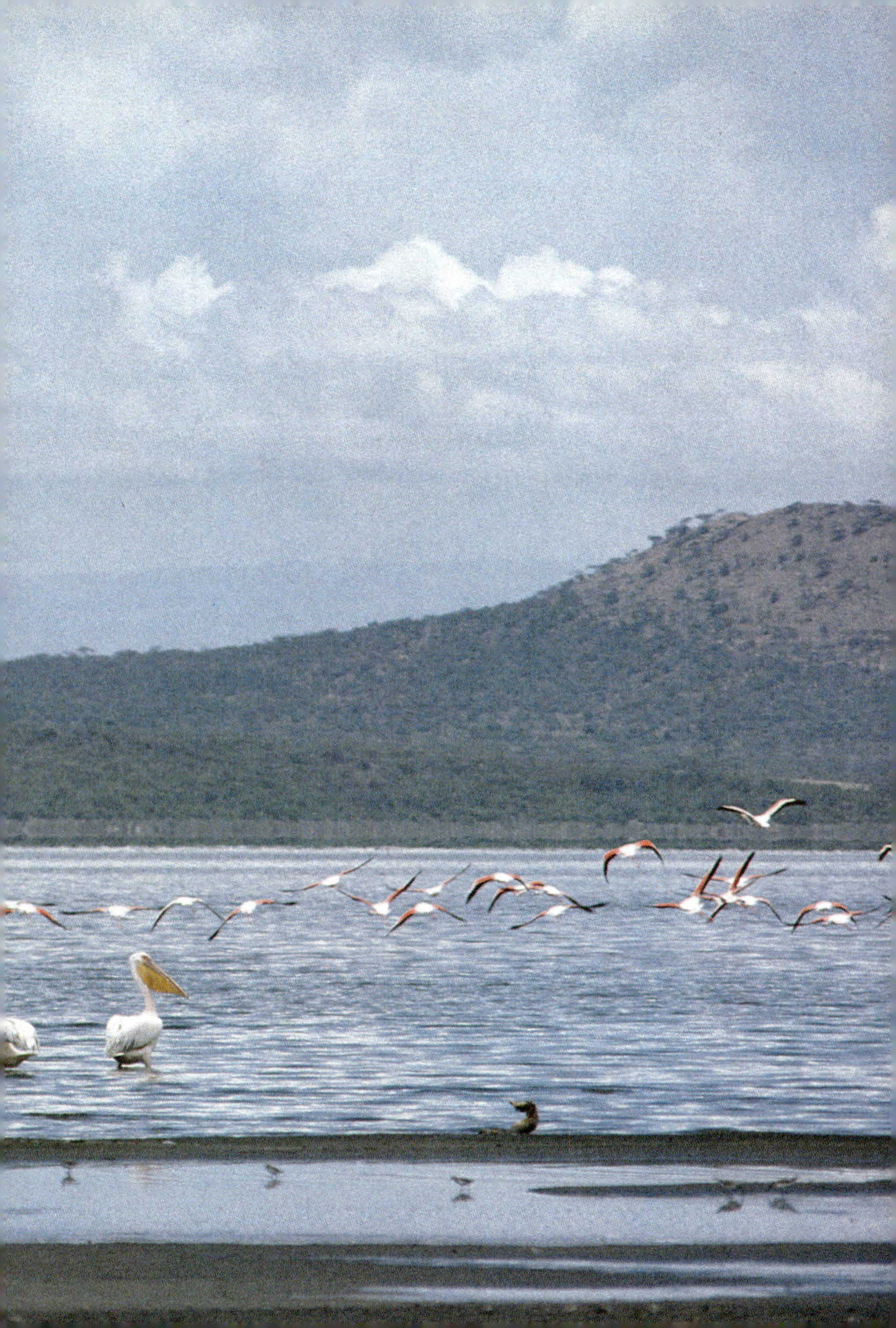

Chapter 4 · Nature and Wildlife

There are six main regions in the world set aside by conservationists as animal sanctuaries. Africa, south of the Sahara, is one of them because of its unique flora and fauna.

Ethiopia, in a sense, is a microcosm of the entire sub-Saharan environment because of the huge variety of its ecosystems, terrain and geography. The Dallol area in the Danakil Depression, where the temperature can rise to 50° C — and which is more than 100 metres below sea-level — shimmers with yellow and blue deposits of potassium. In sharp contrast are the 4,500 metres high, snow-capped Simien Mountains, and the arid Horn of Africa, both of which are rich in very different flora and fauna. The alpine Bale plateau boasts sparkling streams and the largest expanse of moorland in Africa. Also to be found in Ethiopia are colourful gorges deeper than the Grand Canyon; arid moonscapes with unique plant life and land formations; impenetrable jungles; and apparently endless plains and savannahs. There are also wonderlands of lakes, rivers, hot-springs, geysers, volcanic areas spouting steam, and untouched forests.

Africa used to be known as the 'Dark Continent'. However, considerable areas have now been so much explored and developed that 'the back of beyond' of 60 years ago is today traversed by numerous trucks, mini-buses and cars on well-worn routes. The wondrous spectacles of wildlife in many African national parks are now becoming more and more circumscribed by areas of human habitation, and are, consequently, becoming less and less the natural wonder they used to be.

The era of freshness and discovery is now, alas, over — or nearly so. Ethiopia is the sole exception. Here the wilderness remains virtually unchanged since time began and 'the back of beyond' still exists in plenty — in the mountains, in the savannahs and in the awesome deserts of the lowlands. Anyone who travels here in any direction will discover that he is breaking ground that few, other than the indigenous inhabitants, have ever been over before. There is the excitement of discovery in every footstep. The range, number and habitat of many Ethiopian birds, mammals, and other species of wildlife are still imperfectly known. "For those with a taste for something unusual, Ethiopia presents a call to adventure and provides an opportunity to find something new. There are remote areas rich in wildlife. Ethiopia has more large species of mammals than any East African country." So wrote the well-known naturalist, the late Dr Leslie Brown, who contributed much to the campaign to save the Walia ibex from extinction and who played a vital role in the UN declaration of the stunningly beautiful Simien Mountains as a World Heritage Site. At the same time also, a study financed by the EEC in 1981 considered the Omo Valley to be of paramount importance because it had long been recognised as a unique remnant in East Africa of untouched wildlife and wilderness.

Ethiopia's geographical location and remarkable physical features have endowed it with a rich and varied natural heritage of vegetation and wildlife. Its avifauna, for example, is one of the most diverse and abundant in Africa. Some 835 species of birds are found in Ethiopia, of which 26 are exclusive to Ethiopia. So far the existence of 103 species of mammals has been recorded in Ethiopia. Among the endemic mammal species are the Walia ibex, the Simien red fox, the Mountain nyala, the Gelada baboon, the Somali wild ass, Menilek's bushbuck and Swayne's hartebeest.

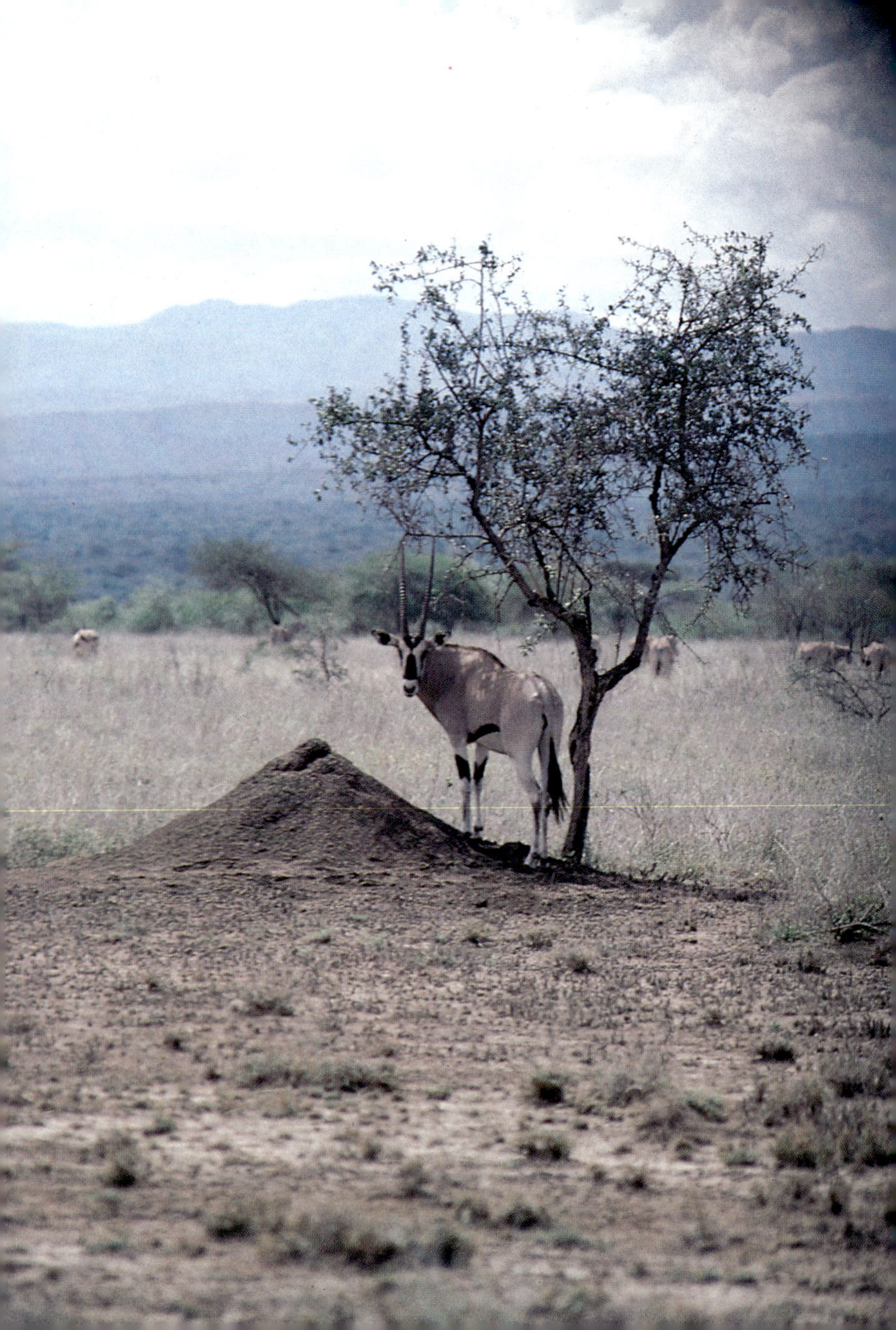

Opposite: Beisa oryx are seen in several of Ethiopia's National Parks.

Below: Palm Springs, in Awash National Park, where hot-springs feed pools of turquoise water.

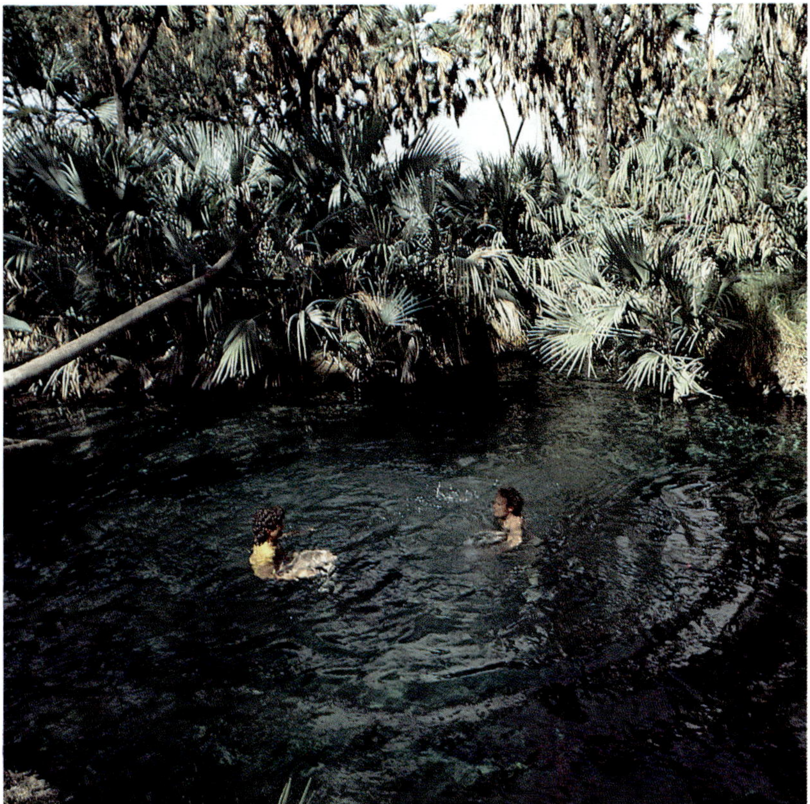

The Walia ibex is found only in the Simien Mountain massif, while the Gelada baboon can also be found in other highland areas. It is to protect these rare species that the Simien Mountain National Park was established. The rare and shy Somali wild ass ranges over the Danakil area to the north-east. The Bale Mountains National Park is the home of the Simien red fox (found in larger numbers there than in the Simiens), the Mountain nyala, and Menilek's bushbuck. Ethiopia's seventh endemic animal, Swayne's hartebeest, is restricted to the Nechisar National Park straddling the southernmost two of Ethiopia's Rift Valley lakes, Chamo and Abaya.

There are pockets of wildlife and utter wilderness in all regions of Ethiopia. Generally speaking, however, the main wildlife concentrations occur in the southern and western half of the country, where most of the national parks, wildlife reserves and controlled hunting areas are located. In total there are nine national parks at various stages of development, 14 wildlife reserves and 14 controlled hunting areas. Some of the most accessible parks are:

AWASH NATIONAL PARK

The Awash National Park is the oldest and most developed game reserve of its kind. It is bordered by the Awash River and lies some 225 kilometres east of Addis Ababa on the Assab highway. The 1,800 metres high semi-dormant Fantalle volcano, an extensive area of pools of mineral hot-springs fringed with doum palms, and the extraordinary phenomenon of rocky blisters (Hawaii is said to be the only other place on earth where these volcanic features are seen) are some of the attractions of this park. The wildlife consists mostly of East African plains game with the exception of giraffe and buffalo. The oryx, the bat-eared fox, the caracal, the aardvark, colobus and green monkeys, Anubis and Hamadryas baboons, the klipspringer, the leopard, the bushbuck, the hippo, the Soemmerring's gazelle, the Grevy's zebra, the cheetah, the greater and lesser kudu . . . and 400 species of birds are to be found within the 756-square-kilometre area of the Awash National Park.

BALE MOUNTAINS NATIONAL PARK

Surprisingly enough it is not to the Simien Mountains that one should go to see the Simien red fox. The fox is now more abundant, and more easily seen, in the Bale Mountains National Park which covers 2,470 square kilometres.

With their vast moorlands, their lower reaches covered with St John's wort, their extensive heath, their virgin woodlands, their pristine mountain streams and with their alpine climate, the Bale Mountains are a beautiful world all of their own. Rising to a height of over 4,000 metres, the Bale mountain ranges border the southern highlands of Ethiopia. Mount Batu, the second highest peak in Ethiopia, is 4,307 metres high.

The establishment of the Bale Mountains National Park was timely in saving the Mountain nyala, Menilek's bushbuck and the Simien red fox — one of the most beautiful and colourful members of the wolf family. All three endemic animals thrive in this environment and the nyala in particular can be seen in large numbers. The creeks of the park — which become important rivers further down — are well stocked with rainbow and brown trout, introduced there from Kenya in the 1960s.

GAMBELLA NATIONAL PARK

The Baro River area, accessible by land and air through the western Ethiopian town of Gambella is unlike any other region

Below: Carmine bee-eaters are birds of the plains. Often spotted perched on the backs of cattle, game and even of larger birds, they wait to catch insects flushed from the grass.

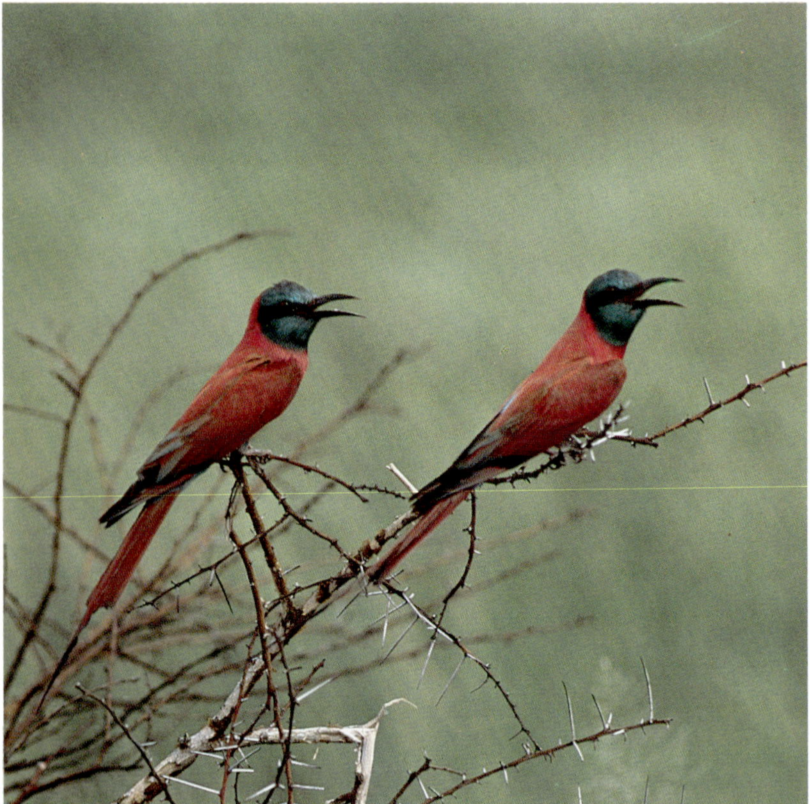

Below: A Baglafecht weaver with its black mask. These birds weave basket-like nests from grasses. Colonies of nests can be seen weighing down the branches of trees in the Rift Valley Lakes area.

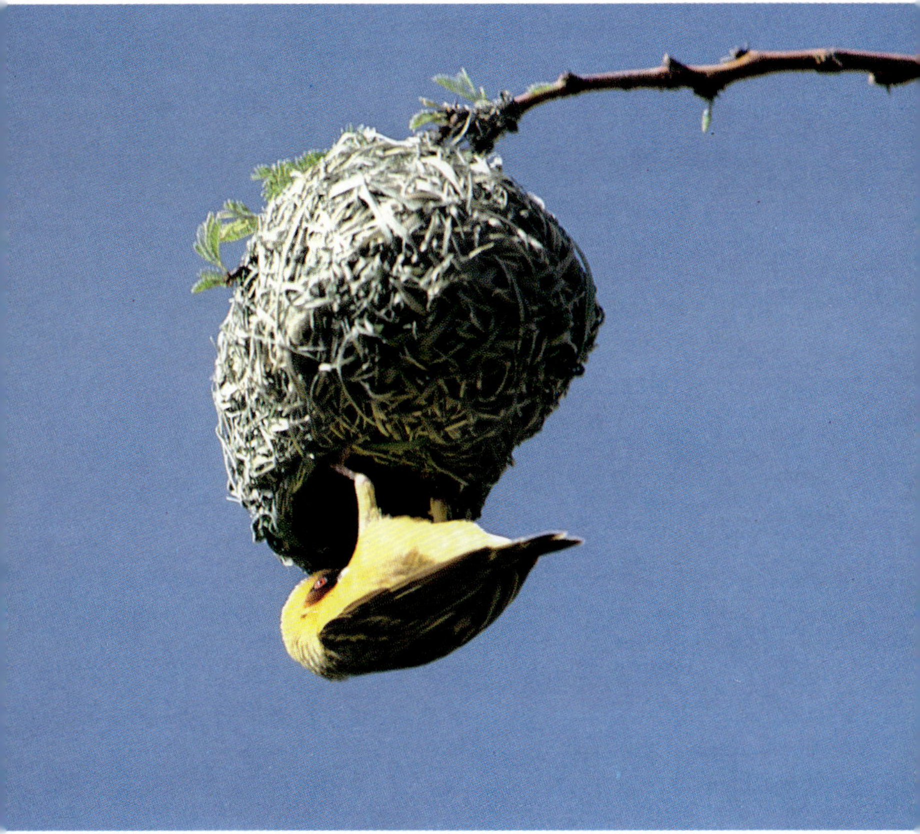

in Ethiopia. It is a place of exciting adventure and one of the few remaining challenges to the explorer. Lost in the endless undulating plains of high Sudanese grass, the traveller can enjoy a sense of achievement in just finding his way. This is Ethiopia's true tropical zone and here all the elements of the African safari are to be found, enhanced by a distinctly Ethiopian flavour. The park, the largest in the country, covers 5,060 square kilometres.

Nile perch weighing over 100 kilos have been caught in the waters of the Baro, and huge crocodiles thrive here on such fare. The rare white-eared kob is found here, along with the Nile lechwe, buffalo, giraffe, tiang, waterbuck, roan antelope, zebra, bushbuck, Abyssinian reedbuck, warthog, hartebeest, lion, elephant and hippotamus.

OMO NATIONAL PARK

The Omo National Park is situated in the remote south-west of Ethiopia. It is adjacent to the Omo River, which flows southwards into Lake Turkana supplying 92 per cent of its waters. The park is one of the richest and least visited wildlife sanctuaries in eastern Africa. The eland, the oryx, Burchell's zebra, Lelwel's hartebeest, the buffalo, the giraffe, the elephant, and more common species like the waterbuck, the kudu, the lion, the leopard and the cheetah may be seen in great numbers. If one is lucky, one may also spot a pack of wild dogs.

The Omo Valley is virtually free from human habitation, except along the banks of the river. The Omo National Park, the third largest in the country with an area of 4,068 square kilometres, is a vast expanse of true wilderness.

The Omo Valley — including the park area — is rich in palaeoanthropological remains. According to the 1982 findings of scientists of the University of California at Berkeley, the latest hominid remains from the Omo Valley are probably over four million years old.

SIMIEN MOUNTAINS NATIONAL PARK

In the earth's long history of violent geological changes, the most recent volcanic upheavals took place in eastern Africa. The region's torrential rains created many gushing waterfalls, which in turn eroded away the newly-formed mountain massifs, creating the great gorges and gullies so typical of the area. The Simien Mountain massif is a broad plateau, cut off on the north and west by an enormous single crag over 60 kilometres long. To the south the table land slopes gently down to 2,200 metres, divided by gorges 1,000 metres deep that can take up to two days to cross. Not enough geological time has elapsed to smooth the contours of the crags and buttresses of hardened basalt. As far as the eye can see (looking north from the escarpment), the fused volcanic cores jut up starkly, defying the elements. Overhead stretches the vast dome of sky of the deepest blue, which spreads downwards as clear as sapphire to the mauve of the horizon.

In this spectacular splendour are to be found the Walia ibex, the Simien red fox, and the Gelada baboon (three of Ethiopia's endemic animals). Other species include the Hamadryas baboon, the klipspringer and the bushbuck, as well as birds like the lammergeyer (the famous bone-breaker), the Auger buzzard, Verreaux's eagle, the kestrel and the Lanner falcon.

The Simien Mountains National Park covers 179 square kilometres of highland area at an average elevation of 4,000 metres. The highest peak in Ethiopia and the fourth highest in Africa, Ras Deshen, which rises to 4,453 metres, stands adjacent to the park.

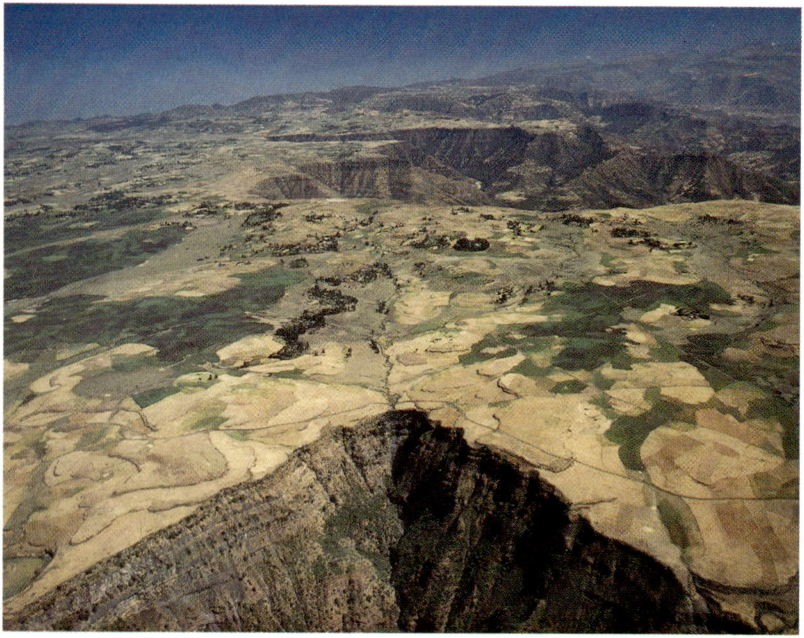

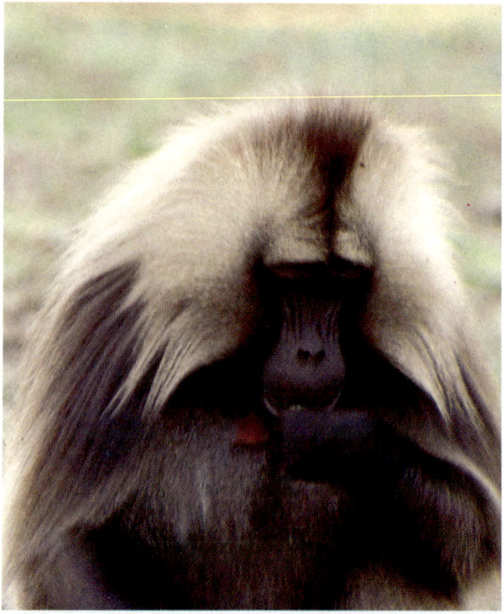

Above: Simien Mountains escarpments.

Left: A Gelada baboon, an endemic mammal found in the Simien Mountains.

Opposite: Giant lobelia, an alpine plant that after 25 years of slow vegetative growth suddenly produces a 10-metre high flowering stalk.

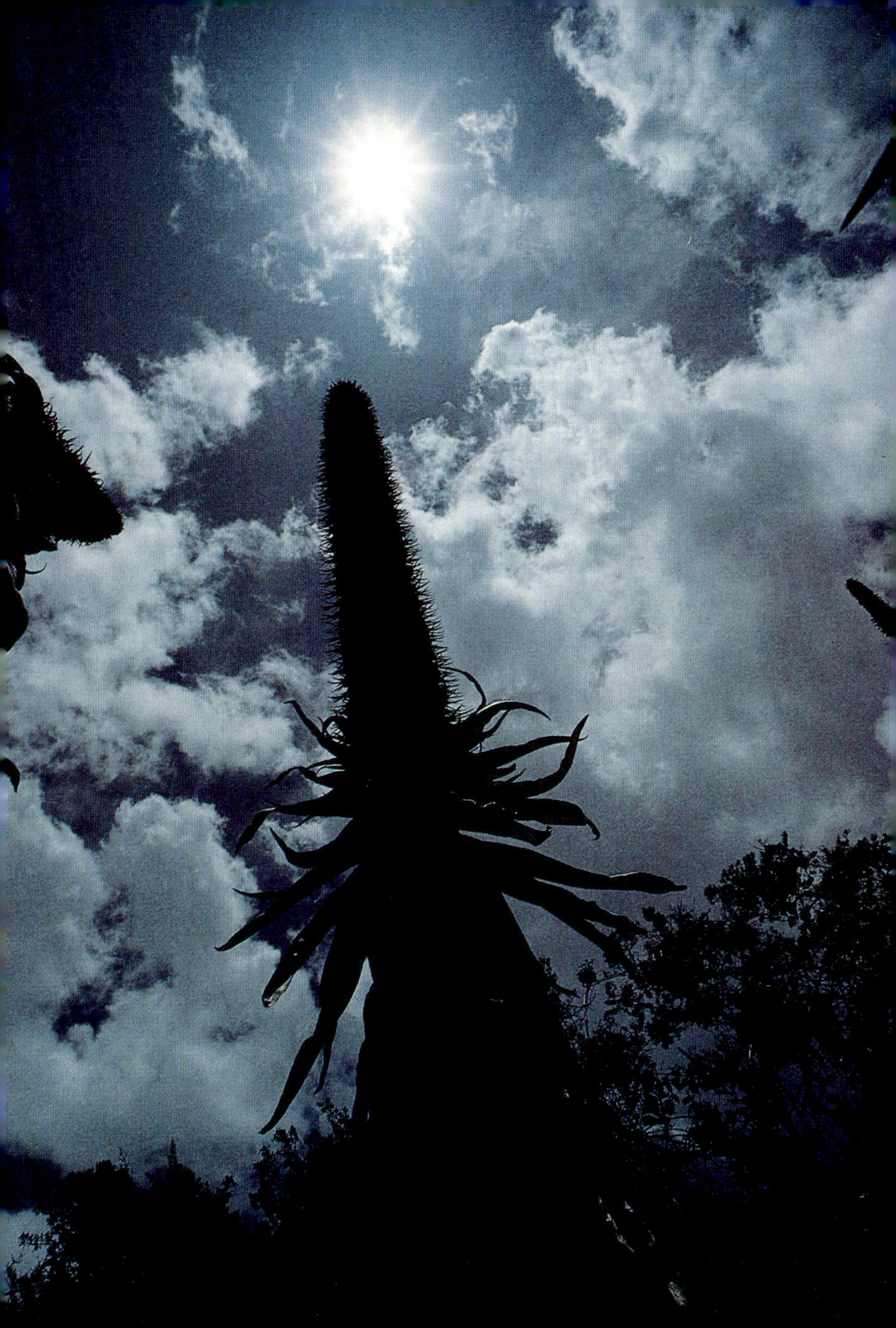

The park is situated 120 kilometres north-east of Gondar, the castle-city of Africa and one of the former capitals of Ethiopia. The Simien escarpments, which are often compared to the Grand Canyon of the United States of America, have been adopted by UNESCO as a World Heritage Site.

The other national parks are Mago (2,162 square kilometres) 770 kilometres southwest of Addis Ababa on the Omo River; Nechisar National Park (574 square kilometres) in the southern Rift; and Yangudati-Rassa National Park (4,730 square kilometres), 500 kilometres northeast of Addis Ababa.

RIFT VALLEY LAKES

Much of Africa's volcanic activity is concentrated along the immense 2,800 kilometres-long crack in the earth's surface known as the Rift Valley — without doubt the greatest valley in the world. The valley is the result of two roughly parallel faults in the earth's surface between which, in distant geological time, the crust was weakened and the land subsided.

Ethiopia is often referred to as the 'water tower' of eastern Africa because of the many rivers that pour off the high tableland. The Great Rift Valley's passage through Ethiopia is marked by a chain of lakes fed by these rivers. Numbering seven in all, the Rift Valley lakes each have their own special life and character and provide ideal habitats for the exuberant variety of flora and fauna that make the region such a delight for naturalists and tourists.

Lake Zwai

The northernmost and largest of the chain, Zwai is a shallow freshwater lake. Its extensive aquatic vegetation attracts a

Overleaf: 'Crocodile Market', Lake Chamo. This lake and the Omo River contain some of the largest concentrations of the Nile crocodile in the world.

variety of interesting water birds. Especially common and easy to see are the long-tailed cormorants, darters, and various herons and storks — including the distinctive saddle-bill stork. Wading through the water lilies are long-toed marsh birds such as the black crane and the greater jacana. The handsome African fish eagle perches in the fig-trees along the shore line, throwing back its head to give its haunting, gull-like cry. Green pigeons, black-headed orioles, wood-hoopoes, and barbets are also found here.

Lake Langano

Because of its hotels, camping facilities, and its proximity to Addis Ababa — it is 210 kilometres south of the capital city — the brown-and-copper-coloured Lake Langano is popular for swimming, aquatic sports, sunbathing and for camping. There is also much of interest for bird-watchers. Along the shores of the lake many cliff-dwelling and acacia-inhabiting birds are to be found. Fan-tailed ravens and hornbills — including Hemprich's hornbill whose nesting grounds at Langano were discovered and described for the first time relatively recently — find ideal habitat amongst the surrounding cliffs. In the acacia woodlands helmet-shrikes are to be found in great numbers along with colourful bush butcher-birds, several of whose pairs often combine to build a nest.

Lakes Abyata and Shala

Not far from Langano — and about 215 kilometres south of Addis Ababa — are Lakes Abyata and Shala, situated in the heart of the Rift Valley. The two lakes are exceptionally scenic stretches of water. Lake Shala is shrouded by an aura of primeval wonder, and may also be the deepest lake in Africa

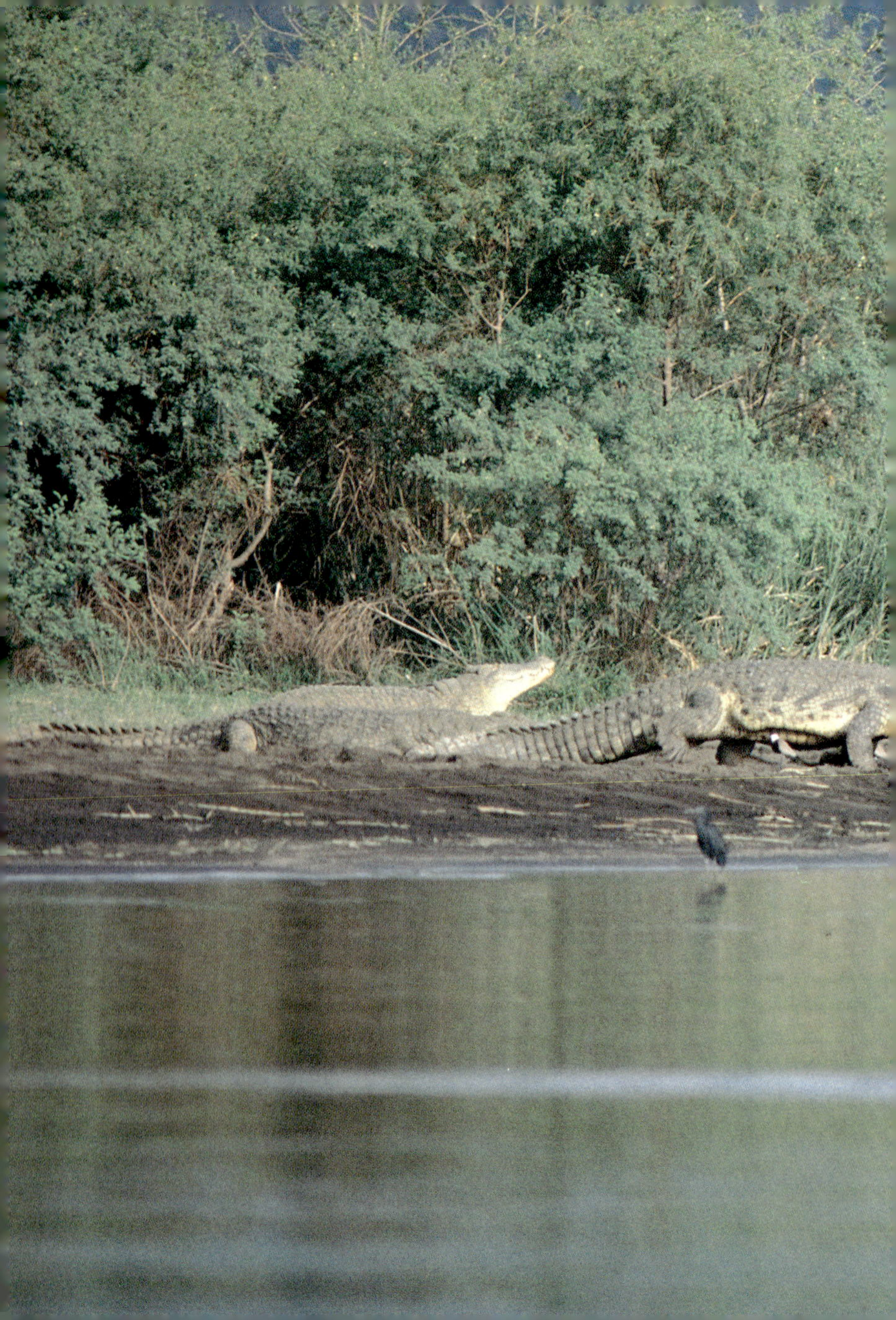

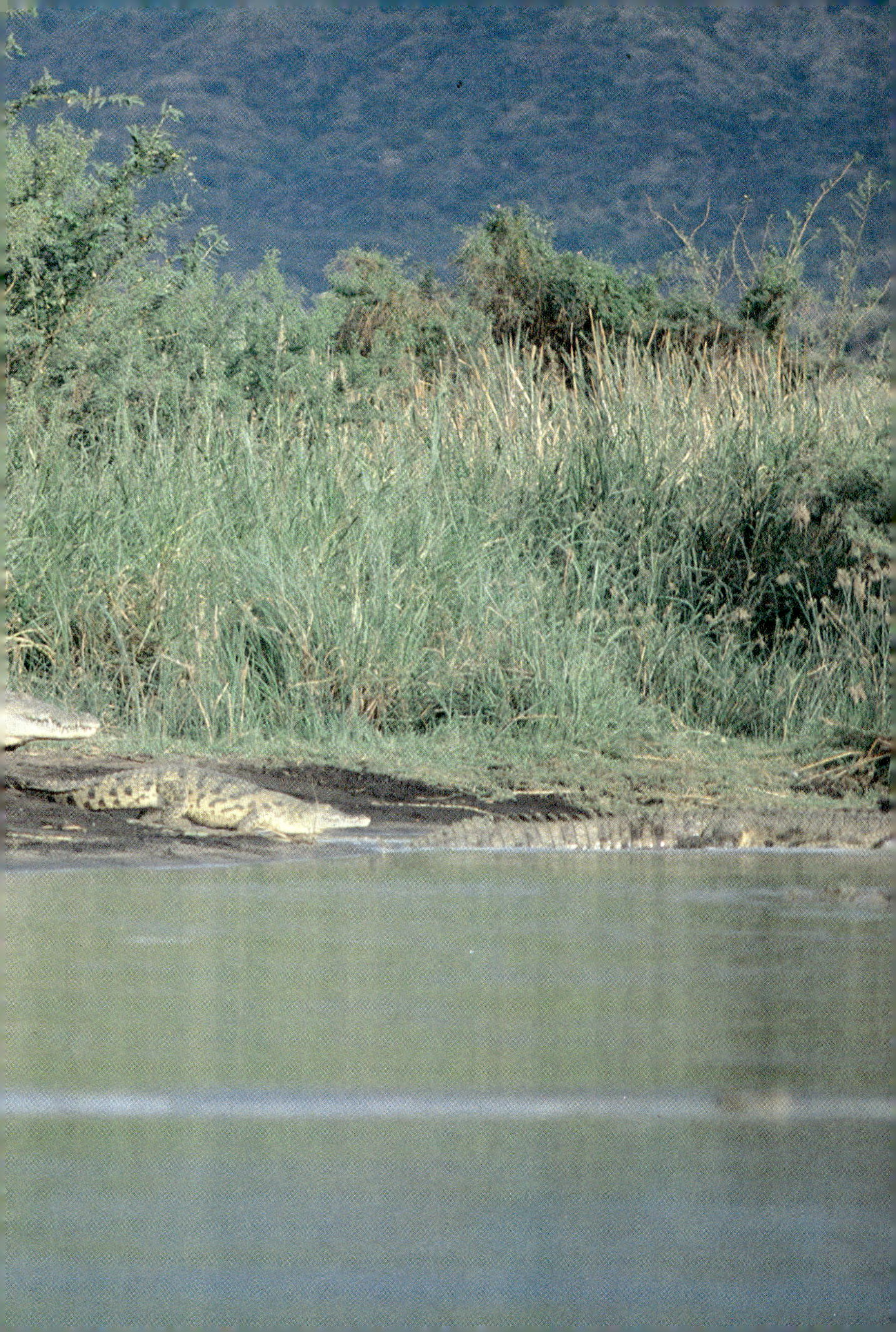

north of the Equator. Lake Abyata, a soda lake, has vast expanses of white shoreline.

But it is for their birdlife that these lakes are best known, with as many as 150 different species found here.

At Abyata greater and lesser flamingos abound, along with white- necked cormorants, great white pelicans, several species of herons, storks spoonbills and ibises — including the sacred ibis (sacred to ancient Egypt) — various species of African ducks, shorebirds, gulls and terns often in their thousands. In addition, during the northern winter, thousands of Asiatic and European ducks and waders migrate to Abyata's shores.

Lake Shala is well-known for its large colony of great white pelicans — undoubtedly the most important breeding colony for this species in Africa. The sacred ibis, Abdimi's stork and the white-necked cormorant are also found here in abundance.

Although the bird colonies of both these lakes are protected from human disturbance, most species can readily be observed at Abyata where they regularly fly from their breeding grounds to feed. The acacia woodlands, cliffs, and riverine forests also provide excellent environments for bird-watching — forests being especially good for trogons, turacos and weavers.

Lake Awasa

When it comes to the aesthetic values of lacustrine peace and serenity, Lake Awasa — lying just south of the town of Shashamane — is peerless. A gentle chain of mountains and a low plateau surround the lake, opening to a wide, low bay in the south. Swampy bays interspersed with volcanic rocks, sandy shores with bare rocky hills, and every formation of terrain imaginable can be found near Lake Awasa. The lake teems with a great variety of fish, and, as elsewhere in the Rift Valley, there are many species of birds.

Lakes Abaya and Chamo

The two southernmost of the chain of Ethiopia's Rift Valley lakes, Abaya and Chamo are the lushest in vegetation and the richest in wildlife.

The lakes support many species of fish — including the Nile perch and the tiger fish — and hordes of hippos and crocodiles. Local people call one spot on the western shores of Lake Chamo *Azo Gabia,* or 'Crocodile Market', because of the huge numbers of crocodiles to be seen there. One should take a good look at an Ethiopian country market to appreciate the accuracy of this analogy.

The Nechisar National Park embraces the eastern shores of Lakes Abaya and Chamo. Nechisar was established as a sanctuary for Ethiopia's seventh endemic animal — Swayne's hartebeest — an endangered species.

The bluff between the two lakes — locally known as the 'Bridge of Heaven' — is carpeted with luxuriant vegetation and gives life to numerous springs. The town of Arba Minch — meaning 'forty springs' — takes its name from these gushing streams.

Below: All Rift Valley lakes offer spectacular sunsets.

Opposite: Lake Hora, one of the beautiful crater-lakes surrounding the town of Debre Zeit.

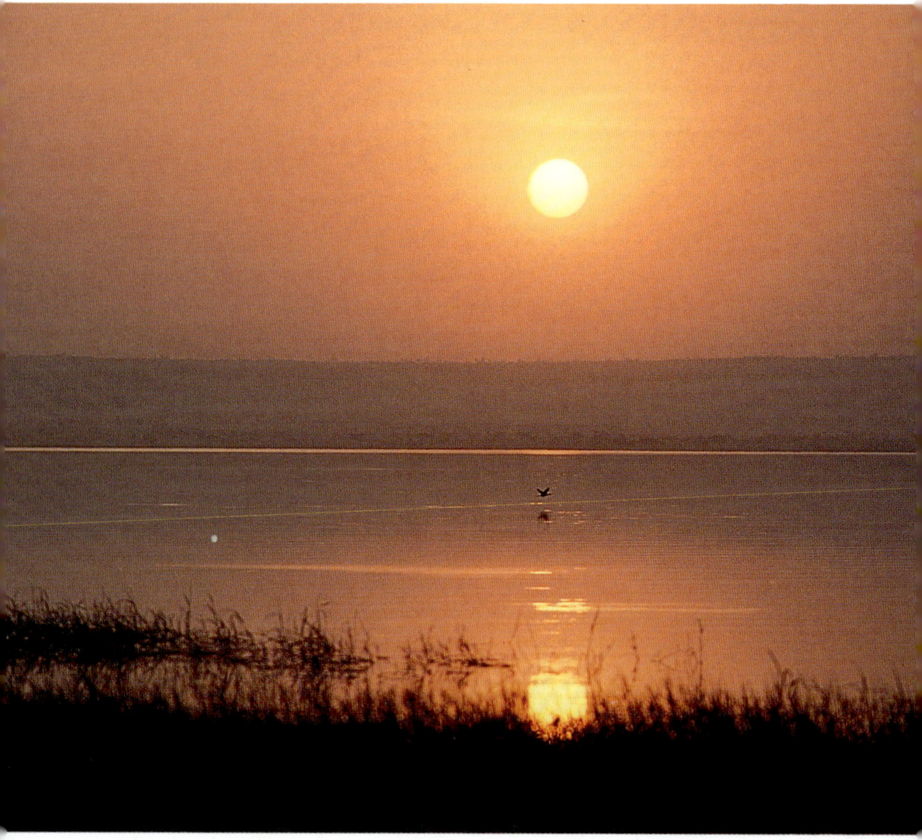

Opposite: Sodere Filwoha, a popular spa about 125 kilometres south of Addis Ababa.

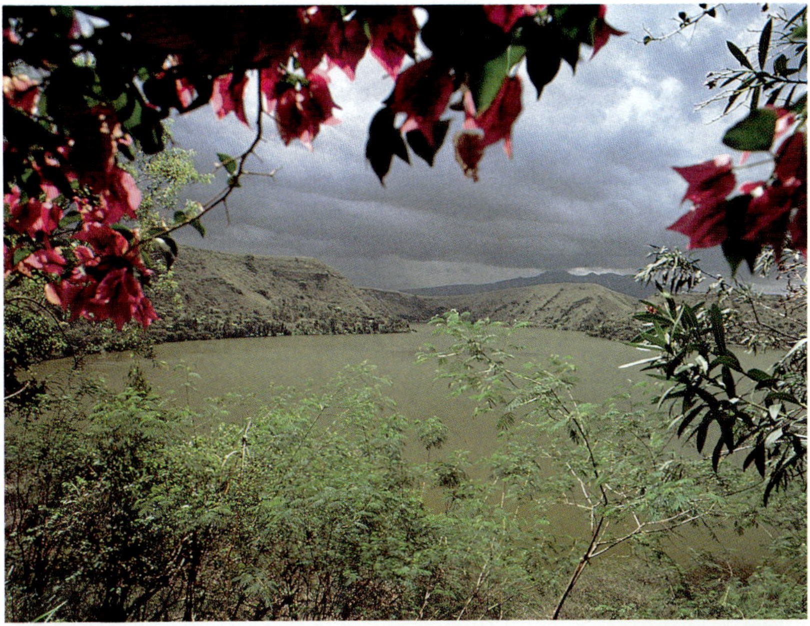

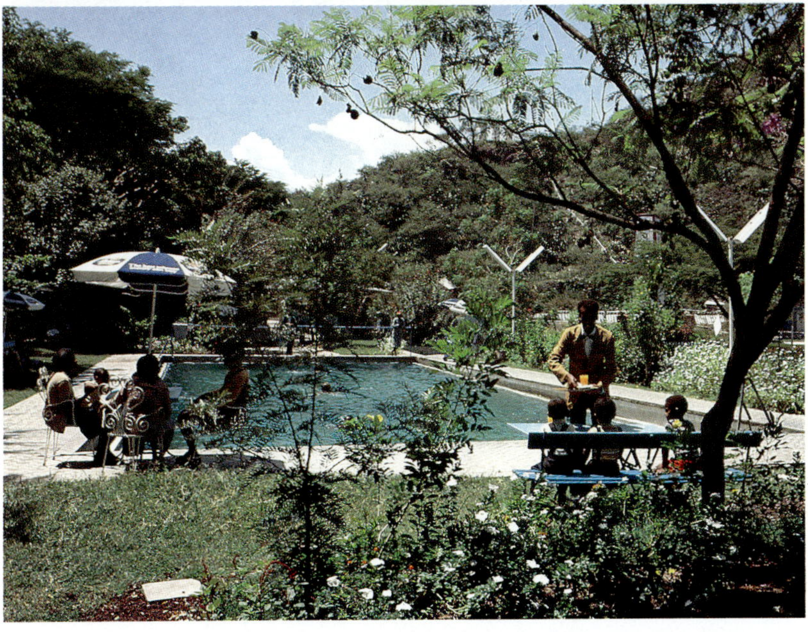

Chapter 5 · Towns and Cities to Visit

ADDIS ABABA

With a population of more than two million people, Addis Ababa is not only the political capital but also the economic and social nerve-centre of Ethiopia. Founded by Emperor Menilek in 1887, this big, sprawling, hospitable city still bears the stamp of his exuberant personality. More than 21,000 hectares in area, Addis Ababa is situated in the foothills of the 3,000 metres Entoto Mountains and rambles pleasantly across many wooded hillsides and gullies cut through with fast-flowing streams. The altitude of the city itself ranges from 2,200 metres to 2,500 metres above sea-level.

There was never an urban plan as such for Addis Ababa, and the capital has therefore grown in a very natural way over the years — with no social or economic segregation. Thus, the most modern buildings, gleaming in their marble and anodised aluminium, stand side by side with simple country-style huts surrounded by cattle, sheep, goats and chickens. Millions of eucalyptus trees planted on the hillsides add their characteristic aroma to the fresh mountain air.

Before moving to the present site of Addis Ababa, Menilek had established temporary capitals at six different locations. He built or enlarged each town he lived in, and then moved on and abandoned it to its own destiny. Asked to explain this practice by a Frenchman, Monsieur Mondon Vidaye, Menilek then on the point of abandoning Addis Ababa — is reported to have replied: "Why do I move on each time? For the same reason that my predecessors kept on moving. It is because we have exhausted the firewood of the area — and we have to move on to an area where there is an abundant supply of firewood." The Frenchman suggested to Menilek an alternative to the impermanence of Ethiopian cities — the planting of a fast-growing tree. Menilek said he would be glad to stay in Addis Ababa if he could find a tree that would grow fast enough to meet the city's clamouring demand for fuel. The result was the introduction of the eucalyptus from distant Australia — and this tree is the real secret of Addis Ababa's existence and success. The city — its name translated into English means 'New Flower' — became Ethiopia's first permanent capital since the decline of Gondar. Rules and regulations were laid down in 1907 enabling people to buy and sell land in Addis Ababa. A year later the new capital got its first mayor, and two years later people began to acquire title deeds to their land.

Restaurants in Addis Ababa

There are many restaurants offering various exotic dishes from many parts of the world. Ethiopian food is served at the majority and there are Chinese, Italian, French, Indian, Armenian, Arabic, Greek and many other specialist restaurants. Indeed, it is possible to eat your way round the world without ever leaving Addis Ababa.

Entertainment

There are several cinemas showing international films with English dialogue or sub-titles. Most of these cinemas also stage dramas in Amharic depicting Ethiopia's social and cultural life during different historical epochs.

Shopping

The shops in Addis Ababa are fairly well stocked with almost all consumer goods. The local jewellery, sold by the weight of gold or silver, is in particularly high demand. The main market-place, known as the Mercato has a wonderful range of goods and

Below: View of one of the wide avenues of Ethiopia's capital city, Addis Ababa.

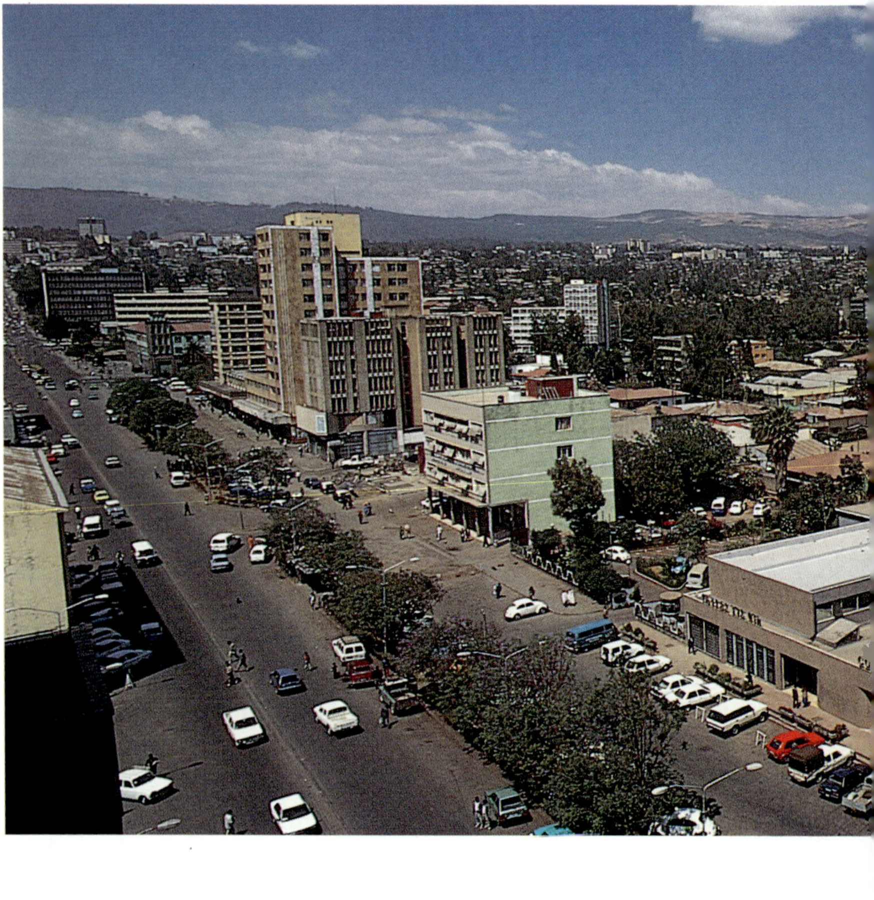

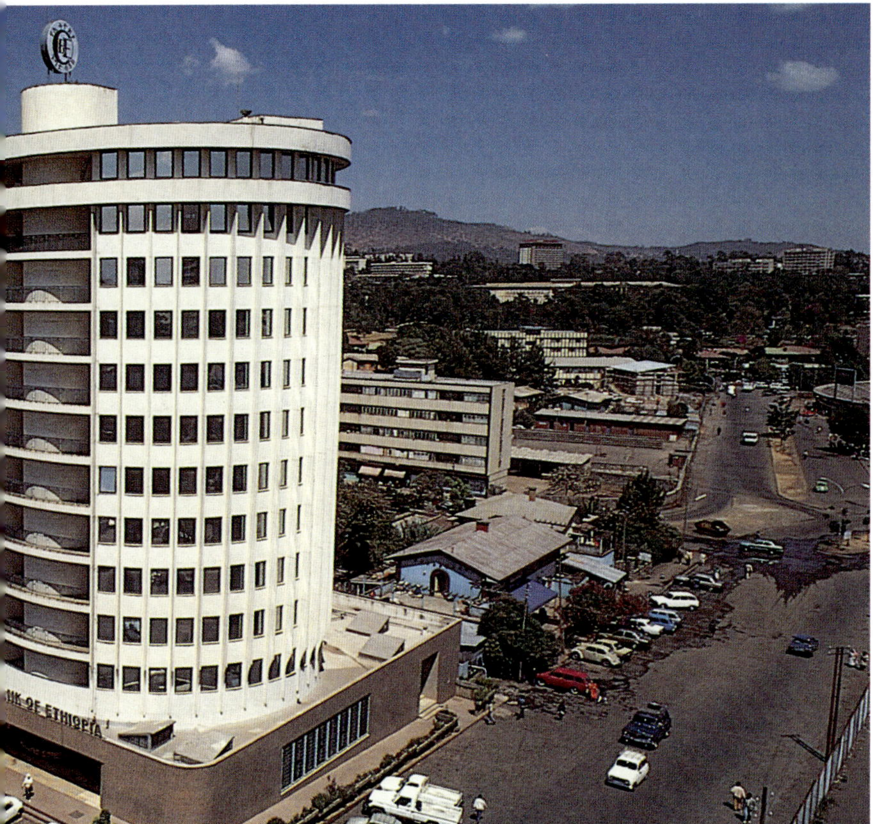
NK OF ETHIOPIA

products, items of local art and Ethiopian curios. Here, haggling over prices is expected — and one should allow ample time for this. At the shops in town, however, prices are fixed, although a small discount is often allowed on large purchases. The Ethiopian Ceramic Workshop supplies kiln-fired pottery in traditional styles.

Places to Visit in Addis Ababa

Addis Ababa University

The main campus of the Addis Ababa University lies in the Sidist Kilo area. This campus occupies a palace and stands in grounds inherited by Haile Selassie from his father. The palace itself was built by Haile Selassie in a modern style, before the Italian occupation of Ethiopia. The Institute of Ethiopian Studies and the Ethnological Museum in the same grounds are also well worth a visit.

St George Cathedral

The St George Cathedral was built in 1896 in the traditional octagonal shape in commemoration of Ethiopia's military success at the Battle of Adwa. (St George is the patron saint of the soldier). The Italians partially burnt it down in 1937; however the Cathedral was restored after the Second World War. It houses modern paintings by Master-Artist Afework Tekle, an Ethiopian painter whose work has won wide international recognition.

Menilek Mausoleum and the Trinity Cathedral

The Menilek Mausoleum was built in 1911 and the Trinity Cathedral in 1941. Both serve as tombs of emperors, princes and Ethiopian martyrs of freedom. Menilek's wife, Taitu, and his daughter, Zauditu, are also entombed at the Mausoleum. The Trinity Cathedral was built to commemorate Ethiopia's liberation from five years of Italian occupation. Its interior resembles that of many European churches. However, its hall is divided into three parts, with two outer aisles and the Holy of Holies in the centre.

The Mercato

The Mercato covers a vast area in western Addis Ababa. It is the largest open market-place in Africa and presents the visitor with a confusing, but fascinating, medley of people and culture. It is divided into areas specialising in various goods and products. The section dealing with Ethiopian arts, crafts, and antiques such as metal crosses in many different designs, manuscript books, old swords, drums and musical instruments, holds the most obvious fascination for tourists. However, the spices on sale in the market, the vegetables, baskets and carpets are also interesting to contemplate in their rich diversity.

Entoto

Addis Ababa lies in the natural amphitheatre of the surrounding hills — the Entoto being prominent among them. When Menilek first came here a century ago his builders originally started work on the chilly and eerie heights of Entoto, before moving down to the comfort of the valley. Little remains of this early town, with the sole exception of the Mariam and Raguel churches, both of which have interesting murals.

Excursions from Addis Ababa

The small town of Bishoftu, or Debre Zeit, is only about an hour's drive south-east of Addis Ababa. It is surrounded by

Below: The Mercato, Africa's largest open-air market, where thousands of people gather.

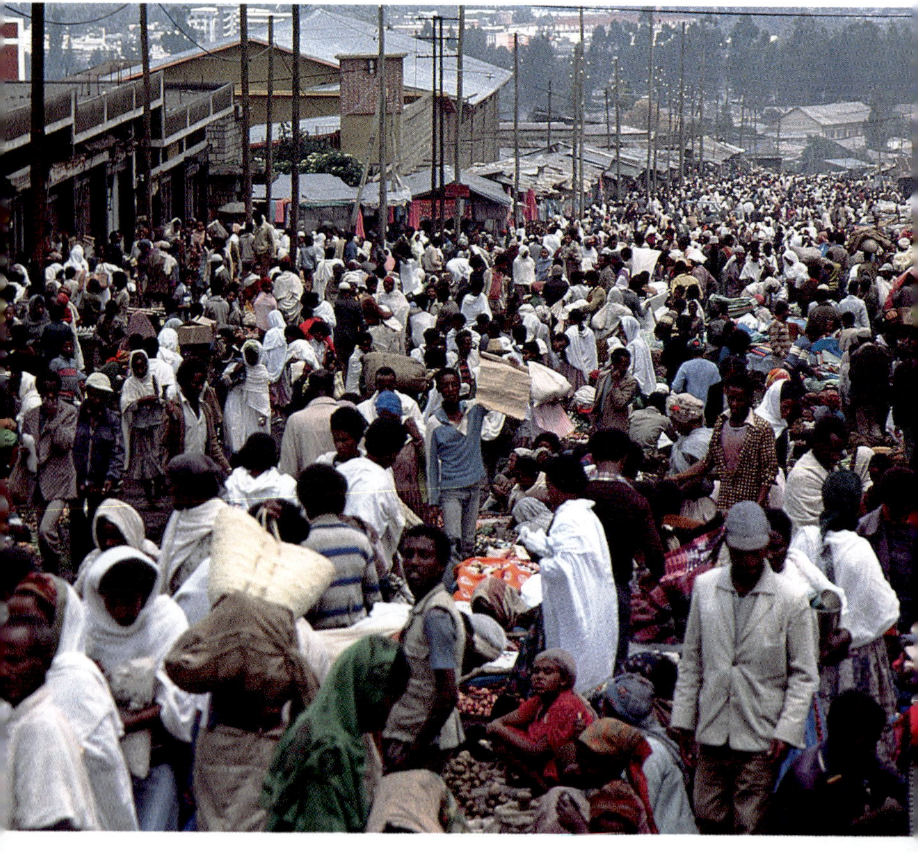

Below: The 23-metre-high standing stele at Axum is carved to represent a tower-house of nine-storeys.

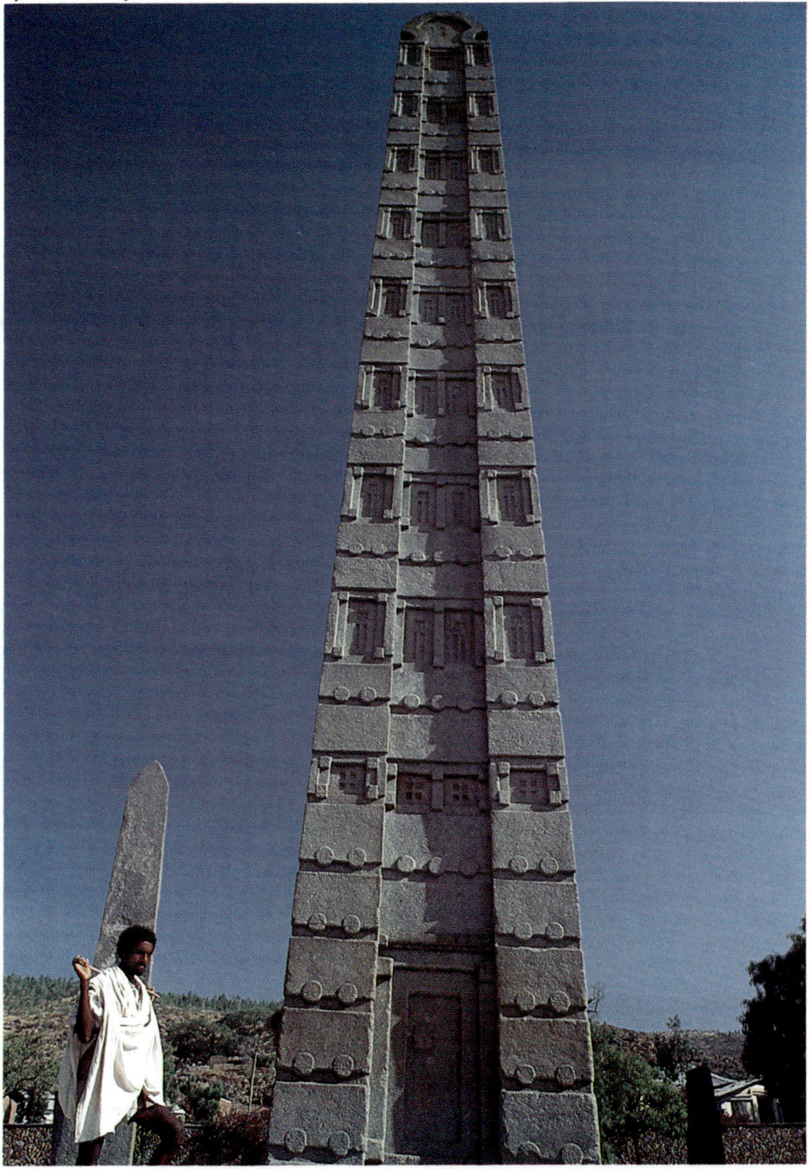

three volcanic crater-lakes which offer swimming, boating and water-skiing.

The Managasha Park lies about 35 kilometres west of Addis Ababa. A mountain forest sanctuary for birds and animals, Managasha is also a favourite weekend resort. Mountain-climbing through the forest to the great crater of Wachacha is also popular.

Ambo, or Hagere Heywot, is situated about 125 kilometres west of Addis Ababa on the same road. It is a popular spa with a hot-spring swimming pool. From here it is an easy excursion to the beautiful volcanic crater-lake of Wonchi, 26 kilometres away along a dirt track in serene surroundings.

A hundred kilometres north of Addis Ababa on the Gondar road is the revered and ancient monastery of Debre Libanos. Founded by St Tekle Haimanot, it is set in spectacular surroundings at the bottom of an immense gorge through which one of the tributaries of the Blue Nile flows. The Abbot of Debre Libanos is regarded as the head of all Ethiopian monasteries and bears the title of *Itchege.*

AXUM

Axum, the site of Ethiopia's most ancient city, is today a small town blissfully ignorant of its glorious past. The 16th-century Cathedral of St Mary of Zion is built on the site of a much older church probably resembling that of Debre Damo, dating from the 4th century AD. Only a platform and the wide stone steps remain from the earlier structure. The Cathedral is the repository of the crowns of some of Ethiopia's former emperors. According to church legend, it also houses the original Ark of the Covenant — thus making St Mary's the holiest sanctuary in Ethiopia.

The most striking relics of Axum are, however, its obelisks or steles, some still standing, some fallen. They are made of single blocks of granite carved in the representation of multi-storey buildings. The tallest, now fallen, stood over 33 metres high and represented a building of 13 storeys. The biggest obelisk still standing is 23 metres high, with 10 storeys. The carving is deep and precise, showing the beams for each floor, and the windows. The style of construction depicted is similar to that still in fashion in Hadramaut in South Yemen.

Other historical sites include the graves of King Kaleb and King Gabre Meskel, the so-called Bath of the Queen of Sheba, and the ruins of the vast Royal Palace over which, unfortunately, the road to Gondar now passes. The market-place has interesting curios and ancient coins for the delight of tourists. The Yeha Hotel is a tourist-class lodge. Reservations must be made in advance.

BAHAR DAR

Bahar Dar nestles in the southern shores of Lake Tana, and is a centre for boating to the islands on the lake and excursions to the Tissisat Falls — the most spectacular waterfall on the Blue Nile river. The monastery of Dek Stefanos has a priceless collection of icons and manuscripts and houses the mummified remains of a number of Ethiopian emperors including Yikuno Amlak (1268-1283), Zara Yaqob (1434-1468) and Fasiladas (1632-1665).

There are monasteries on some 20 other islands and peninsulas on Lake Tana. The nearest to Bahar Dar are Kebran Gabriel (forbidden to women) and Ura Kidanemereth, on the Zegie Peninsula, which is famous for its frescoes.

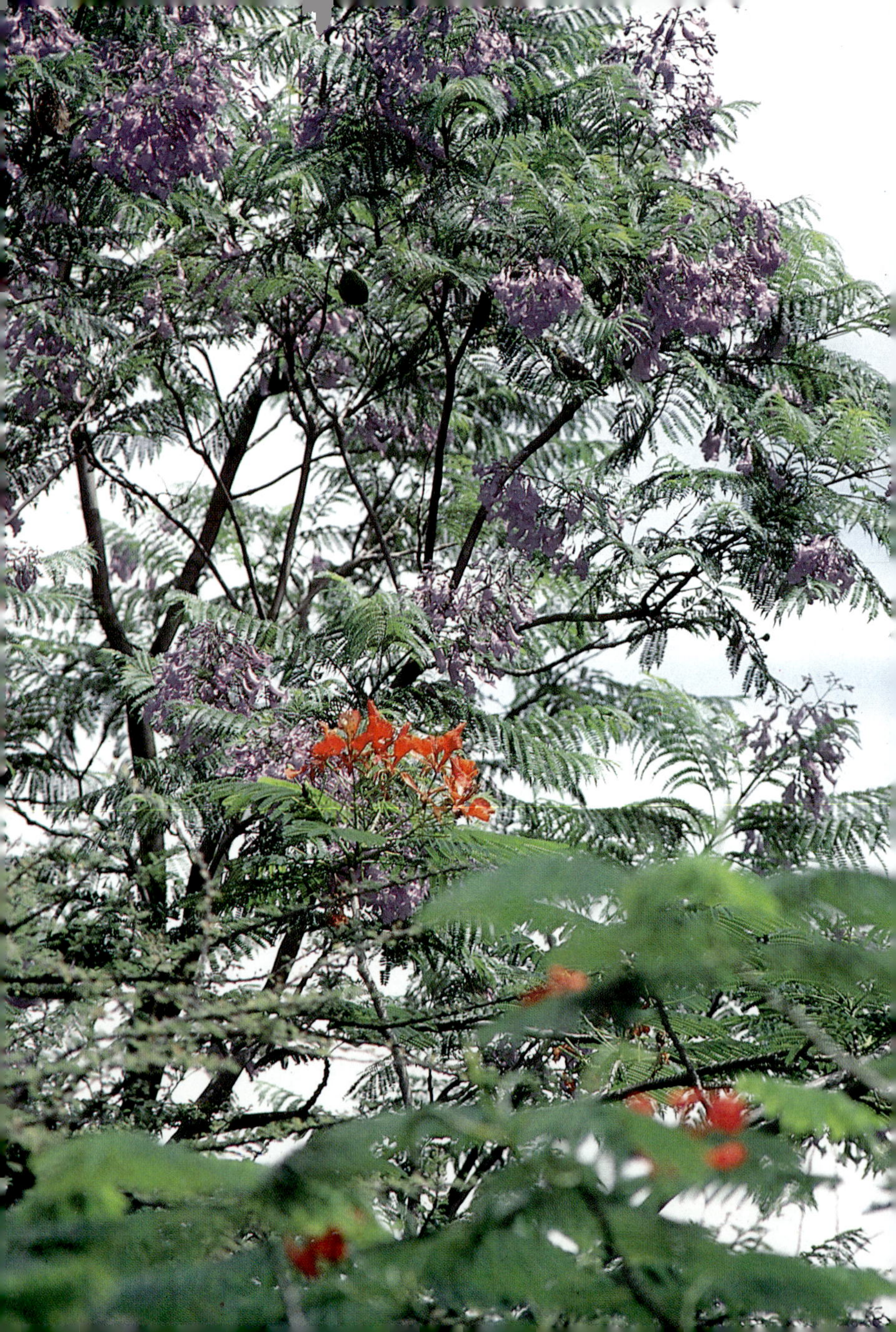

Opposite: Mauve jacaranda and scarlet flamboyant trees line the streets of Dire Dawa.

Below: Priests at the monastery of Ura Kidanemereth on Lake Tana.

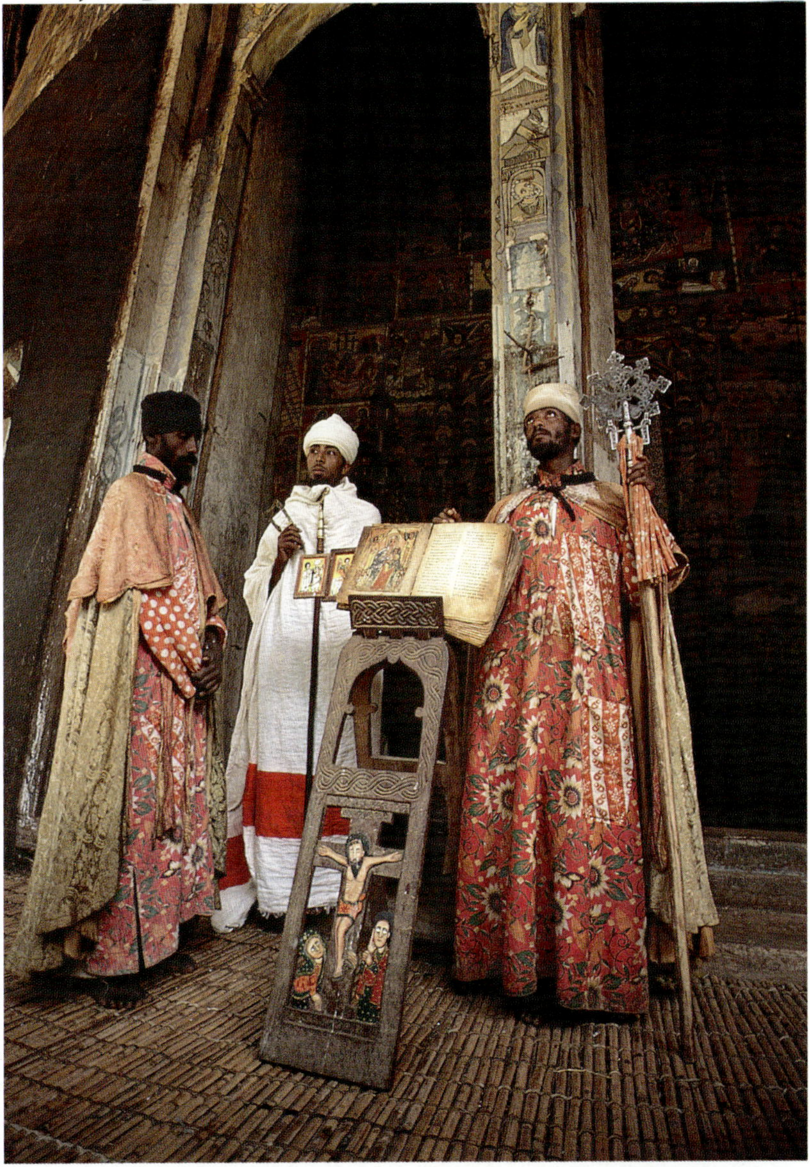

Bahar Dar is a commercial centre of considerable local importance. The large USSR-built Polytechnic Institute and the UNESCO-sponsored Pedagogic Academy are located there.

The Ghion and Tana Hotels offer accommodation and food.

DIRE DAWA

With a cosmopolitan population of 100,000 Dire Dawa lies 517 kilometres east of Addis Ababa — marking approximately the halfway point to Djibouti. Its warm and dry climate contributes to its relaxing and congenial atmosphere. The market-place is frequented by camel-herding Oromos, Somalis, and Afars. There are some caves near the town with prehistoric cave paintings.

There are two fairly good hotels — the air-conditioned Ras, which has a swimming pool, and the Karamara. Dire Dawa has two pleasant open-air cinemas.

GAMBELLA

Empty docks and huge warehouses fallen into disuse are a reminder of the time when the western Ethiopian town of Gambella was a prosperous trading centre and a thriving inland port. The navigable Baro River connects it with Khartoum, 1,388 kilometres away and, because of this, during the late 1940s the British government was permitted to establish port facilities here.

Navigation on the Baro is possible only during the Ethiopian rainy season from June through September. At one time traffic during those months was so heavy that 30 to 40 vessels at any one time could be seen lined up to offload or take on cargo at Gambella. Meanwhile, the Baro Bridge at Gambella, the longest bridge in Ethiopia, completed in 1981, contributed to a transformation of the life of the region.

The landscape, the climate, the vegetation, and the Nilotic peoples — the Anuak and the Nuer — of the lowlands around Gambella are quite unique. The western section of the Ethiopian highland plateau comes to an abrupt end in the province of Illubabor, just beyond the picturesque town of Gore. From here the land falls away rapidly into the Nilotic lowlands of Gambella, going through a series of fast and fascinating changes that impress upon the traveller the intimate nature of the links between lifestyle and geography in Ethiopia.

Descending from the highlands, compressed between high and narrow banks of severe black rock, pouring angrily over rapids, the Baro suddenly loses its momentum as it reaches the lowlands and spreads out into a river-bed of white sand with the banks 100 metres or so apart. Mango and banana plantations intersperse with Anuak settlements of low grass huts while, further downstream, vast grassland plains begin, the only sign of cultivation being sorghum and bean fields close to the river. From here westwards beyond Itang and Jickaw, the Anuak cultivators give way to the pastoral Nuer, whose love of cattle is legendary. Nuer cattle camps into which whole herds of longhorns are gathered at night for security make a dramatic and beautiful sight.

There is one tourist-class hotel in Gambella.

GONDAR

Gondar was the capital of Ethiopia from the rise of Fasiladas (1632-1665) to the fall of Tewodros (1855-1868). The city's unique imperial precinct contains a number of castles built by various emperors during that era. Although the earliest of these castles was built by Fasiladas just after the expulsion of

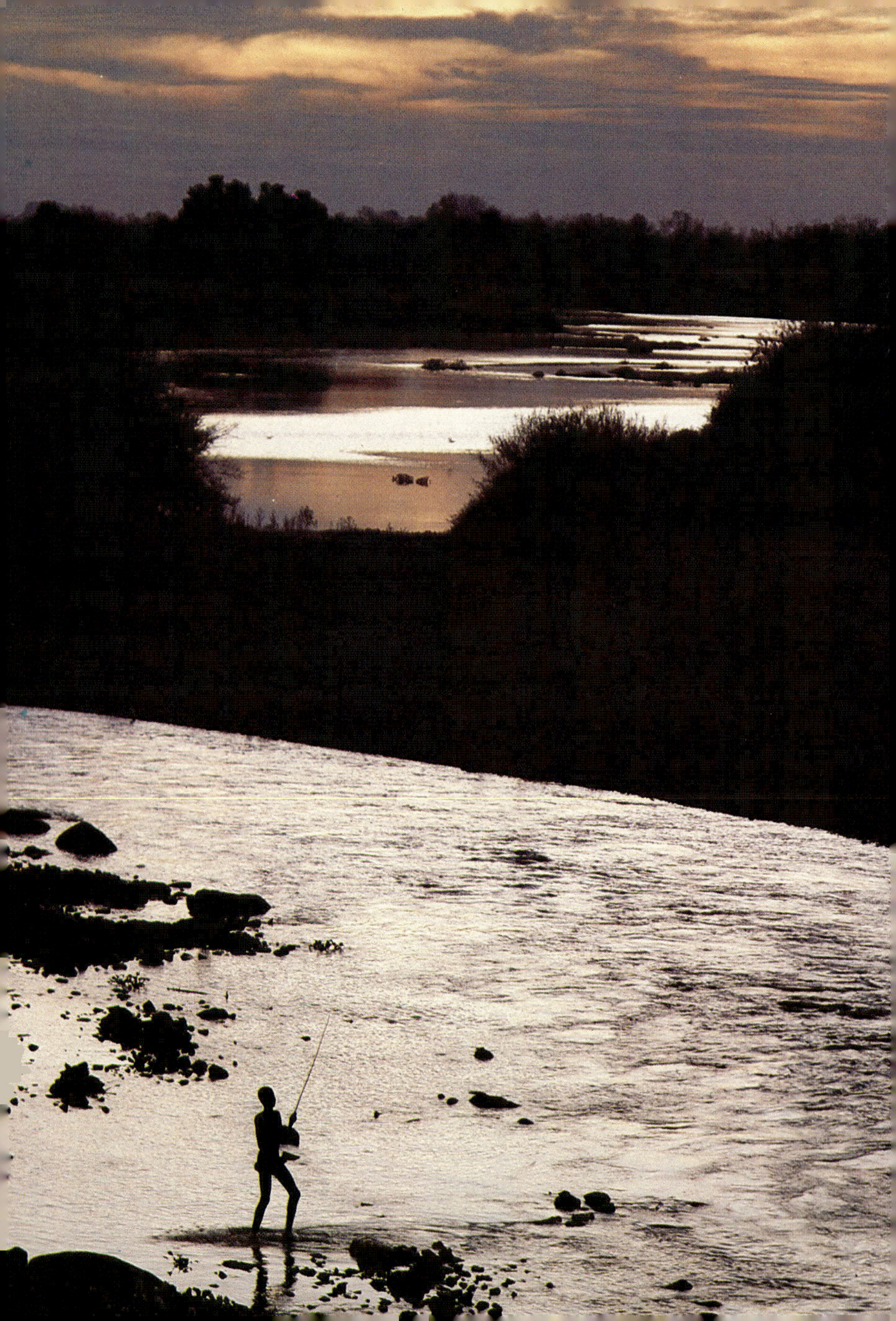

Opposite: Gambella is famous for its dramatic sunsets. View of the Baro river in silver and gold.

Below: Faces of angels painted on the ceiling of Debre Berhan Selassie Church at Gondar.

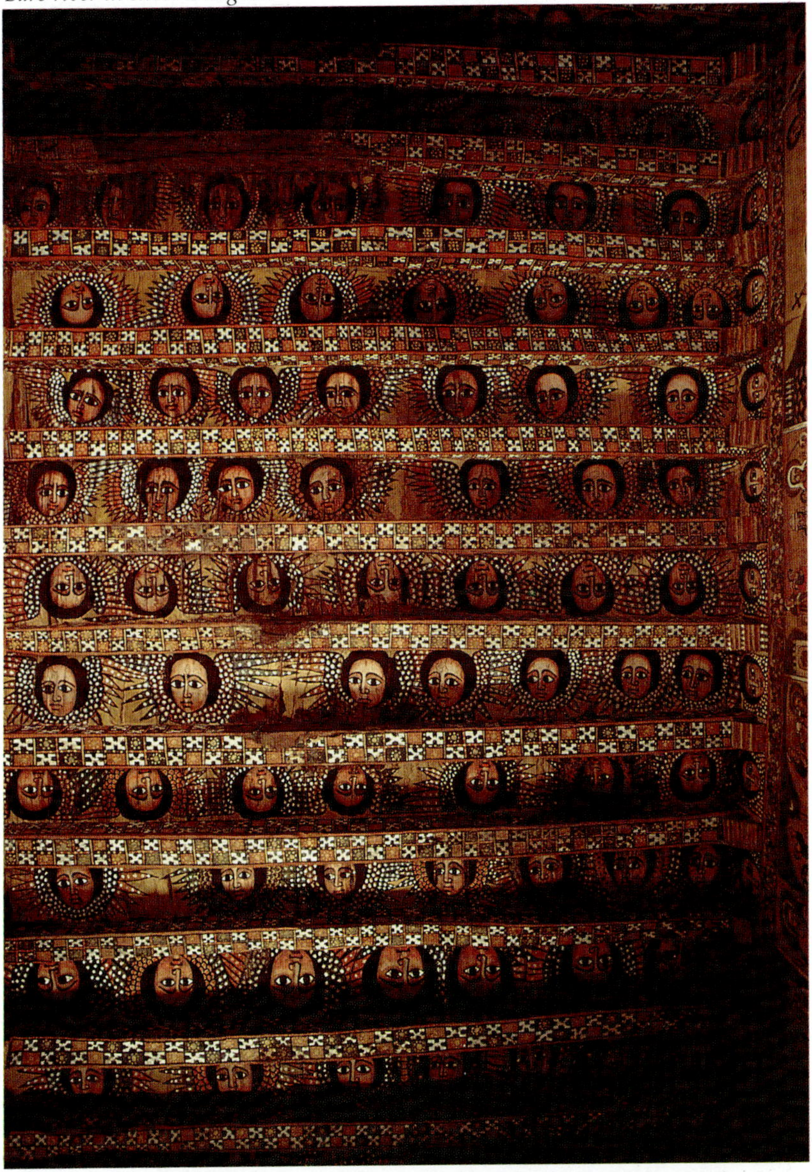

the Portuguese, the architecture at first sight seems to reflect Moorish-European influence. However, closer scrutiny reveals interesting architectural features of the Axumite tradition and a strong affinity with contemporary styles of building fashionable in South Arabia. An aura of mystery still shrouds the intellectual parentage of the ideas and skills behind these magnificent castles.

Elsewhere in Gondar is the palace known as Ras Beit built in the 18th century as the private residence of the famous king-maker, Ras Mikael Sehul — and in continuous use ever since. It now serves as Government offices. A short distance away from it is the Bath of Fasiladas and the so-called House of Chickens.

Within easy access of Gondar lies a monastery, the ruined palace at Kusquam, and the church of Debre Berhan Selassie with its unique murals. The town itself has a lively and interesting market-place.

There are four hotels in Gondar — one luxury-class and three tourist-class.

HARAR

The 54-kilometre drive from Dire Dawa to Harar up the escarpment of the Rift Valley is a memorable experience. The warm desert-like aura of Dire Dawa soon gives way to rolling, rich, green farmlands. The road passes the lakes Adele and Alemaya. Some of Ethiopia's best coffee is cultivated in these highland areas, and a mild stimulant known as *khat* also grows extensively in this region.

Harar was a fiercely religious city from the early days of the expansion of Islam until 1887, when the authority of the central government was restored by Menilek. With its 99 mosques, Harar is considered to be the fourth most holy city of Islam. It was after first seizing Harar that Ahmed Gragn launched his attack on the Christian highlands in 1527. Sir Richard Burton's visit to Harar in 1855 nearly cost him his life, when he found it harder to evade detection there than he had done on his visit to Mecca. The French poet, Rimbaud, also chose Harar as his city of exile from French intolerance.

The whole setting of medieval walls tightly embracing the ancient city, its rich and exciting market-place (probably the most colourful in Ethiopia), its towering and majestic mountains, and its bracing, cool air make Harar an exciting place to visit.

The local Ras Hotel provides first-class catering facilities.

From Harar, the road leads through a scenic valley strewn with weird, wind-weathered rocks, to Jijiga — an important marketing centre.

LALIBELA

The best way to get to Lalibela is by air. One can cover the eight-kilometre distance from the airstrip to the Rocks of Ages in a 45-minute drive by four-wheel-drive vehicle — or a three-hour ride on muleback. The surrounding landscape is amongst the most rugged and awe-inspiring in the country.

King Lalibela is credited with the creation of the 11 rock-hewn churches in the 12th century. Their incredible execution — one cannot say 'construction' as they were carved inside and outside from solid rock — their treasures, and the priests who serve in them, are a living expression of the magnetic fascination of medieval Ethiopia.

During the season of 'big rains' from June through September, the town is inaccessible. A visit during Ethiopian

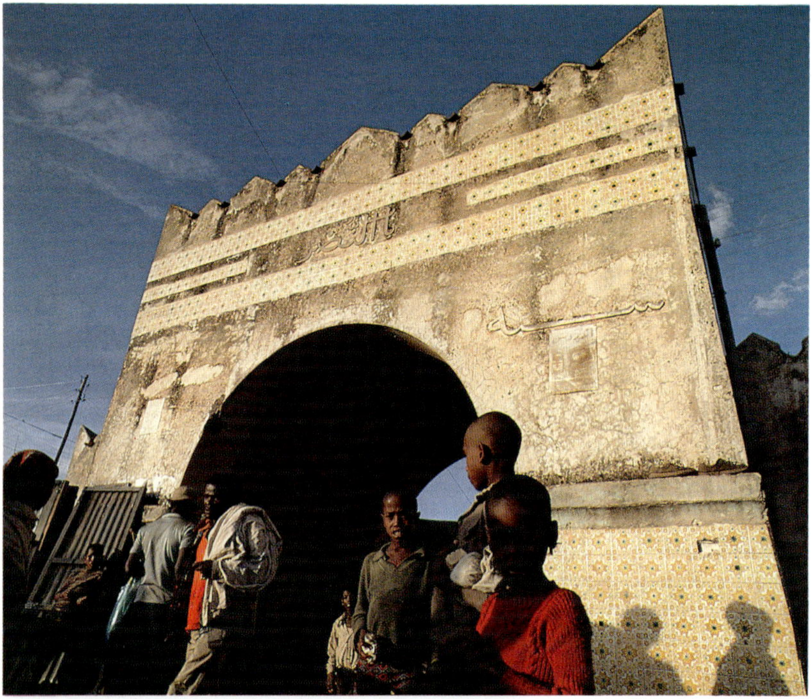

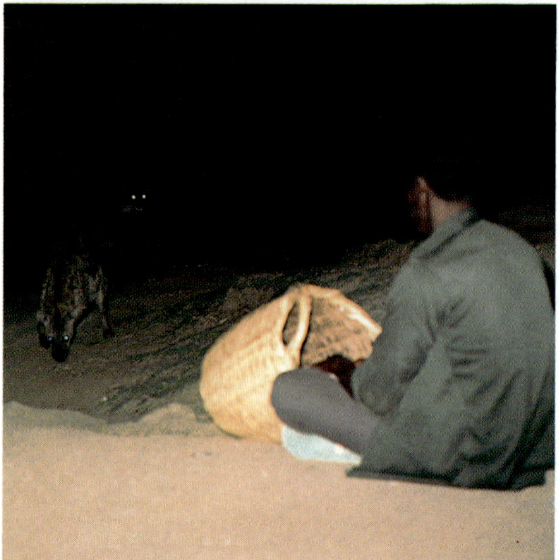

Above: The 'Gate of Victory' at Harar.

Left: Hyena man at Harar, who hand-feeds packs of wild hyenas, offering an unsual spectacle for visitors to the old walled city.

Opposite top: The cross-shaped St George's church at Lalibela.

Opposite bottom: Reached by a stiff climb, the cave-church of Asheton Mariam (top right of picture) high above Lalibela.

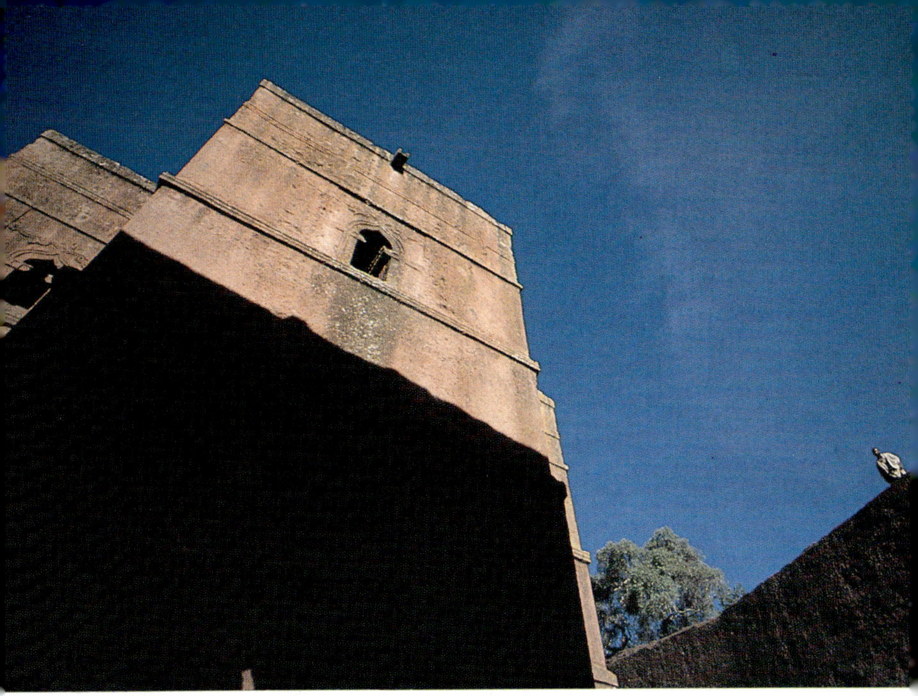

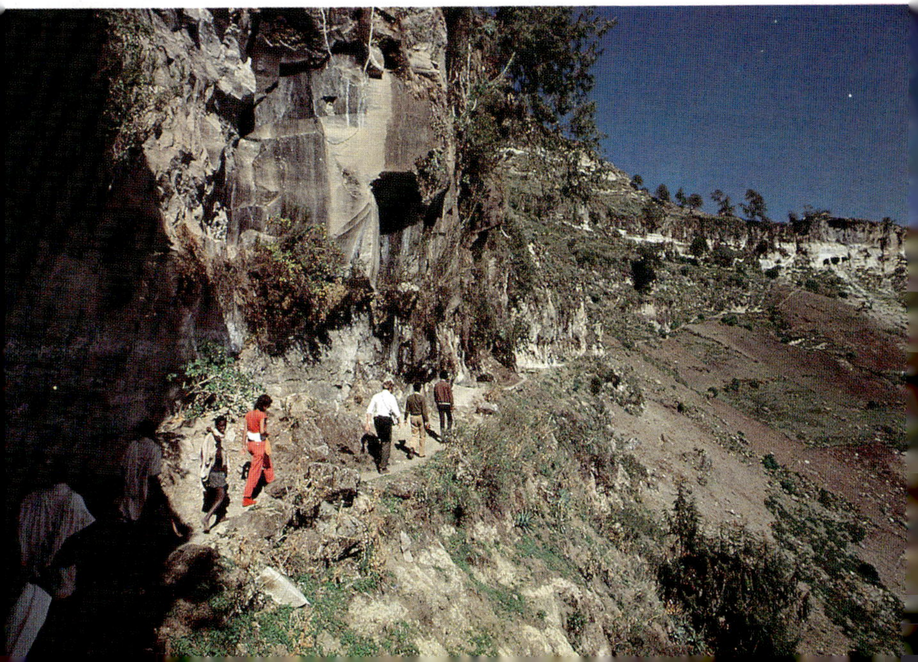

Opposite: Unique circular mural of saints in Tigray's Abune Yemata church.

Easter, Timket (Epiphany) in January, or during some other major church festival is particularly rewarding.

The Seven Olives and the Roha provide excellent hotel facilities.

MAKALE

With a population of 65,000, Makale is the regional capital of Tigray. The old castle in the city has been turned into a small but first-class hotel, the Abraha Atsbaha. It is often fully booked, so advance reservations are advisable.

Excursions to the 130 rock-hewn churches of Tigray can be made from Makale. It is also the spring-board for expeditions to the Danakil Depression, along the ancient salt trail. Makale used to be an important distribution centre for salt from the Danakil.

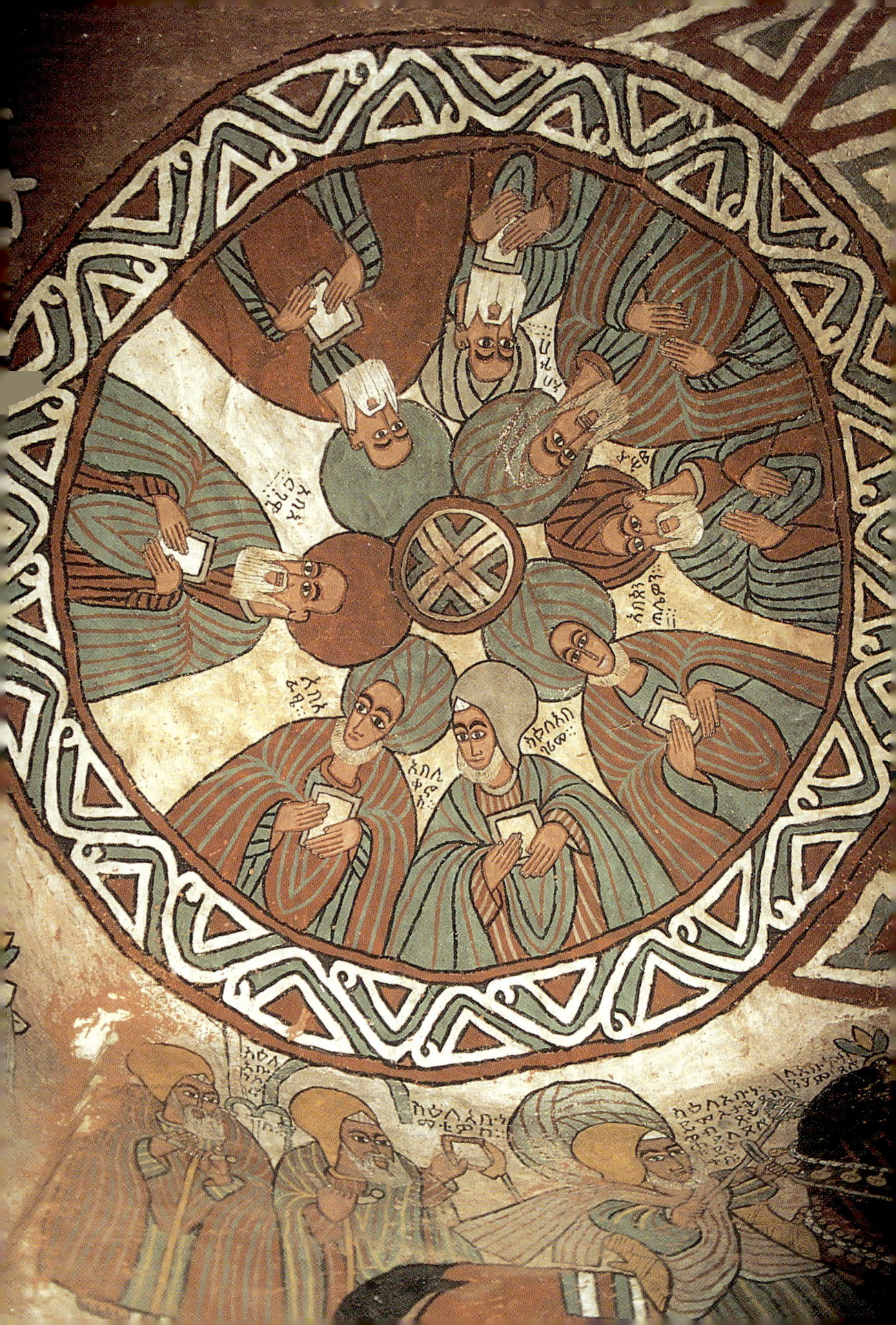

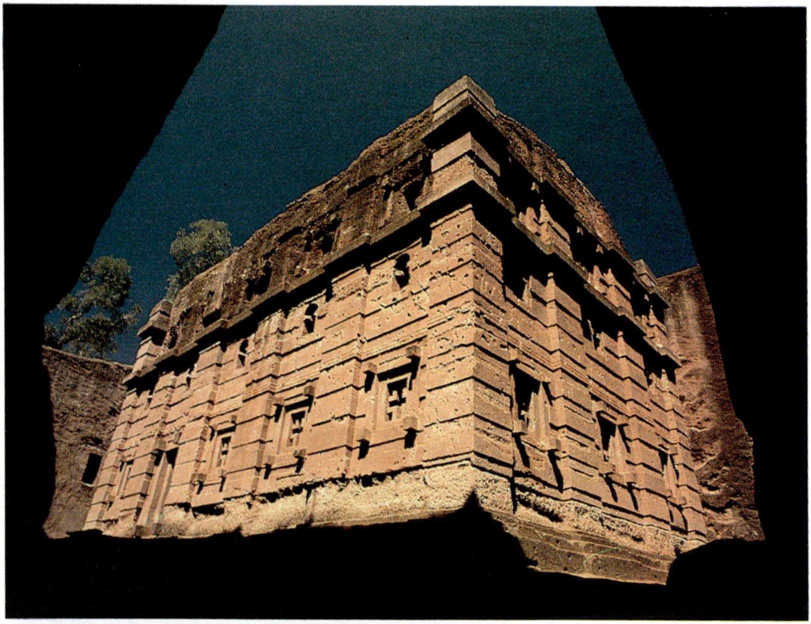

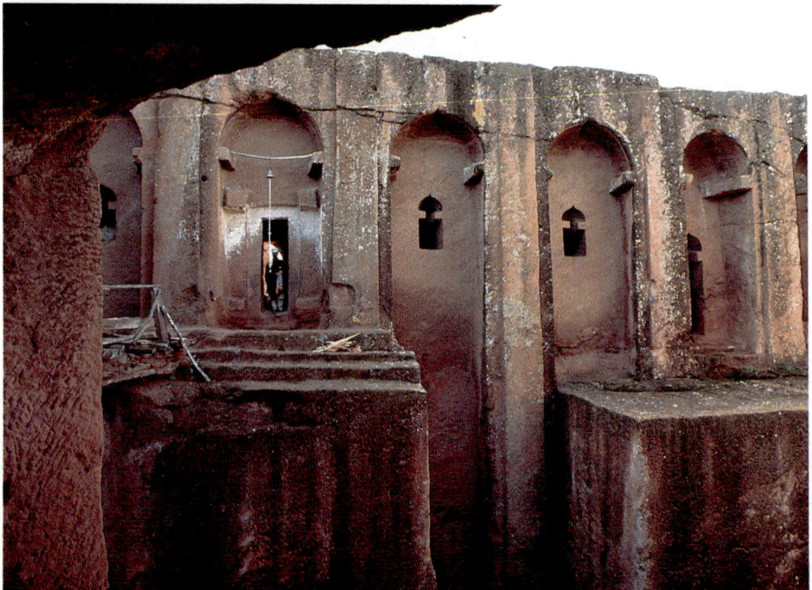

Opposite: Lalibela has eleven facinating rock-hewn churches like this one, built 800 years ago.

Below: Lalibela is set in dramatic mountainous country.

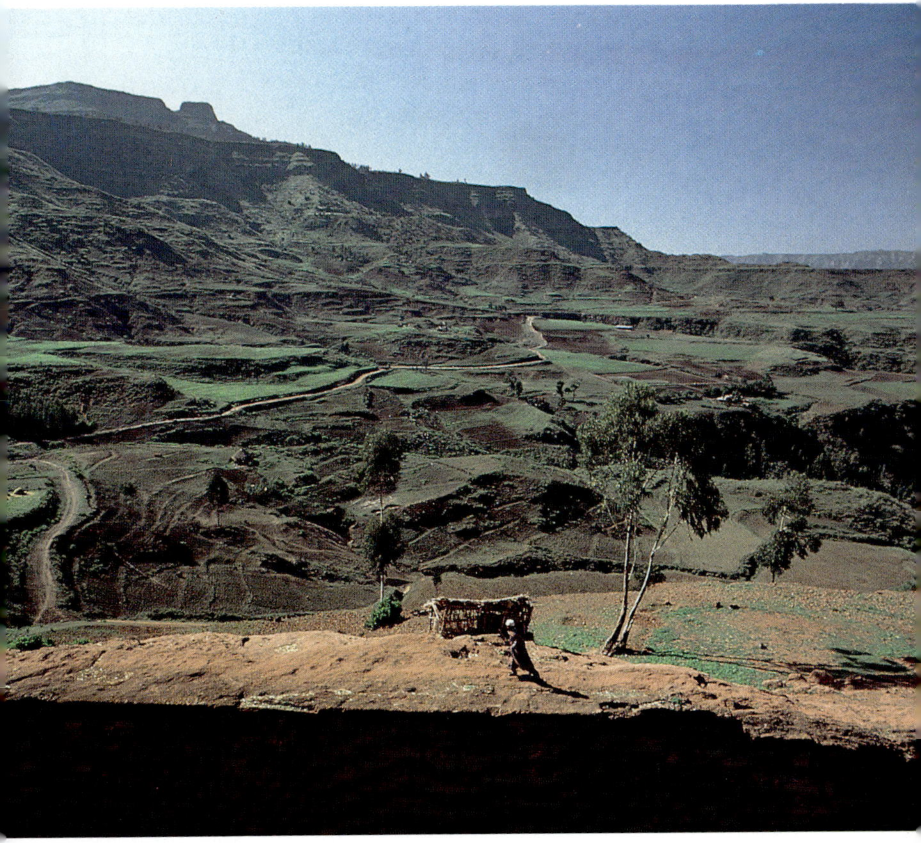

Opposite: The Churches of St. Gabriel and St. Rafael at Lalibela.

Chapter 6 · Useful Tips and Guidelines

Airlines and Air Services

Ethiopia is fortunate in having an experienced and internationally-reputed national carrier. Ethiopian Airlines serves 75 cities in Africa, Asia and Europe. Its domestic service, links 43 airfields and 21 landing strips with the capital city.

Ethiopian Airlines maintains the most modern and comprehensive training schools for pilots and aircraft maintenance technicians in the region. Over 30 airlines utilise these centres for the training of their own employees. Ethiopia is also served by many other airlines.

Addis Ababa's Bole International Airport is able to handle even the largest wide-body aircraft. The airport is about eight kilometres from the city and has a restaurant and duty-free shop. There are also banking facilities and a Tourist Information Desk.

Airport Tax is levied on all departing passengers with the exception of transit passengers.

It is possible to enter Ethiopia by land from Eritrea, Djibouti, Kenya and the Sudan. Dire Dawa and Moyale are secondary ports of entry and exit, but the vast majority of travellers to Ethiopia arrive and leave through Addis Ababa. This occasionally creates a shortage of hotel accommodation during Ethiopia's tourist season from December through May. You can reserve your room in advance through Ethiopian Airlines which has offices or agents in all the major cities of the world, or through travel agents.

Airline Offices and General Sales Agents in Addis Ababa

	Tel:
Aeroflot	51.04.93
Air France	51.90.44
Alitalia	51.44.00
CAAC	65.03.37
Ethiopian Airlines	61.22.22
Kenya Airways	51.30.18
Lufthansa German Airlines	51.56.66
SAS	51.04.37
Saudi Airways	51.77.46
Sudan Airways	51.38.16
Yemen Airways	51.50.76

Air Charter Services

The great canyons of the Simien Mountains, the dazzling salt flats and desolate desert of the Danakil Depression, and the remote wilderness of the Omo Valley make air safaris an exciting adventure in Ethiopia.

Banks

The National Bank of Ethiopia and the Commercial Bank of Ethiopia have their central offices in the same building on Churchill Road. There are also several private banks.

National Bank of Ethiopia
PO Box 5550
Addis Ababa
Tel: 44.17.43

The Commercial Bank of Ethiopia
PO Box 255
Addis Ababa
Tel: 51.50.04

Banks have two sets of hours: cash and business. Cash hours are from 08.00 to 11.00 and 13.00 to 16.00 Monday through Thursday, and from 08.00 to 11.30 and 13.30 to 16.00 on Friday.

Business hours are from 08.00 to 12.00 and 13.00 to 17.00 Monday through Thursday and 08.00 to 10.00 and 13.00 to 17.00 on Friday. All the major banks offer currency exchange.

Currency exchange services are also available at most of the large hotels, which are authorised to exchange convertible foreign currencies into Birr and which can accept convertible currencies in settlement of hotel bills.

Bookshops

The principal bookshops in Addis Ababa stocking foreign-language publications are:

Africa Bookshop
Adua Avenue (opposite the British Council)

Ethiopia Book Centre
King George Street, Arat Kilo

Kuraz Book Centre
King George Street (next to St Mary's Church)
The Kuraz Book Centre also has branches on Meskal Square and at the junction of Gandhi Street and Wavel Street.

Below: Ethiopian Airlines is one of Africa's leading carriers, renowned for its efficiency.

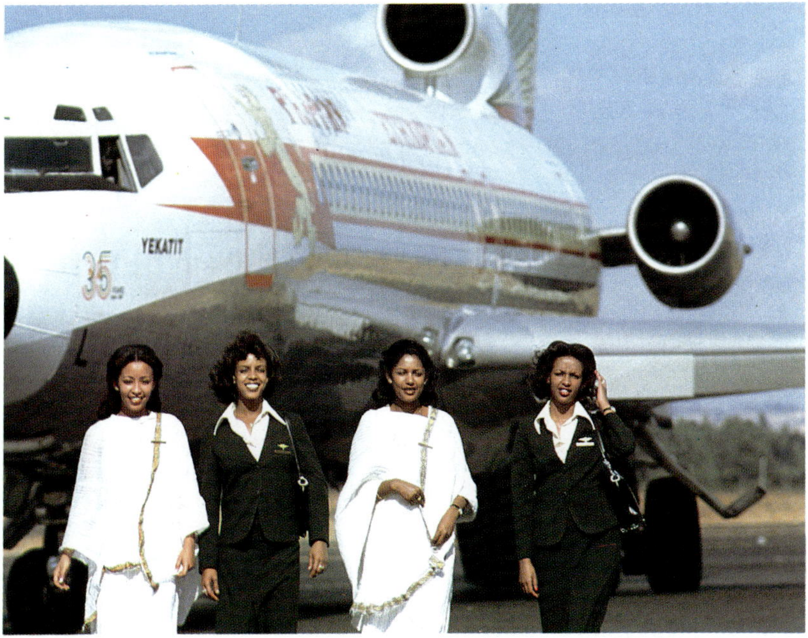

Business Opportunities

Ethiopia is open to foreign investment in several sectors. Policy favours economic cooperation and joint ventures, providing such ventures are deemed to be in the national interest and providing the terms attaching to any investment are equitable.

Ethiopian Chamber of Commerce and Industry
PO Box 517
Addis Ababa
tel: 51.82.40/51.40.05
telex: 21231
Chambercom Addis
fax: 51.76.99

The Investment Office of Ethiopia
PO Box 2428
Addis Ababa
tel: 51.00.33/51.44.43
fax: 51.79.88

Car and Taxi Services in Addis Ababa

National Tour Operation (NTO) maintain large fleets of vehicles ranging from chauffeur driven saloon cars for hire, limousines for airport to hotel transfers, luxury air-conditioned buses for tours and four-wheel-drive safari vehicles.

The cream-coloured NTO Mercedes taxis are stationed outside all the major hotels and at the airport. They have reasonable fixed rates, and a receipt is given for the fare.

The small blue and white taxis that ply around the city are not usually for single-party occupancy hire, nor do they always go where the customer wishes. If you stop one, you should first ask if the driver is going in your direction, and fares must be negotiated at the beginning of your trip.

NTO has offices at the airport and Addis Ababa Hilton, and branches at Axum, Bahar Dar, Dire Dawa, Gondar, Lalibela and Mekele. (Tel: 514838/512923 Fax: 517688).

Private taxis are also available.

Cinemas

Most films are in English with Arabic and French subtitles. There are several cinemas in Addis Ababa, but some of these can be crowded and untidy and are not recommended for tourists. Showings begin at 1630, 1830 and 2100.

Courtesies

A saying from the Ethiopian highlands enjoins that one's home is for entertaining strangers. The same hospitable principle applies throughout the country today, whether in shops, modern offices or a humble hut on a country road. Whatever the traveller's reasons for stopping by, chances are that he will be met first with an eager face and a series of questions aimed at ascertaining his well-being, country of origin and his purpose for visiting. And the next enquiry is likely to be: "Please tea or coffee?" Getting the tea or coffee may take as long as half an hour but you should accept the offer to please your Ethiopian host. And if you are in a hurry to proceed with the business of your call, you will not speed up matters by forgoing the hospitality.

For a people to whom 3,000 years is as close as yesterday, and whose heritage goes back millions of years, time does not march with as much speed as it does for Western visitors.

Below: Addis Ababa's many handicraft shops sell a wide variety of local products.

Opposite: Bargains for the traveller at Addis Ababa Duty-Free shop.

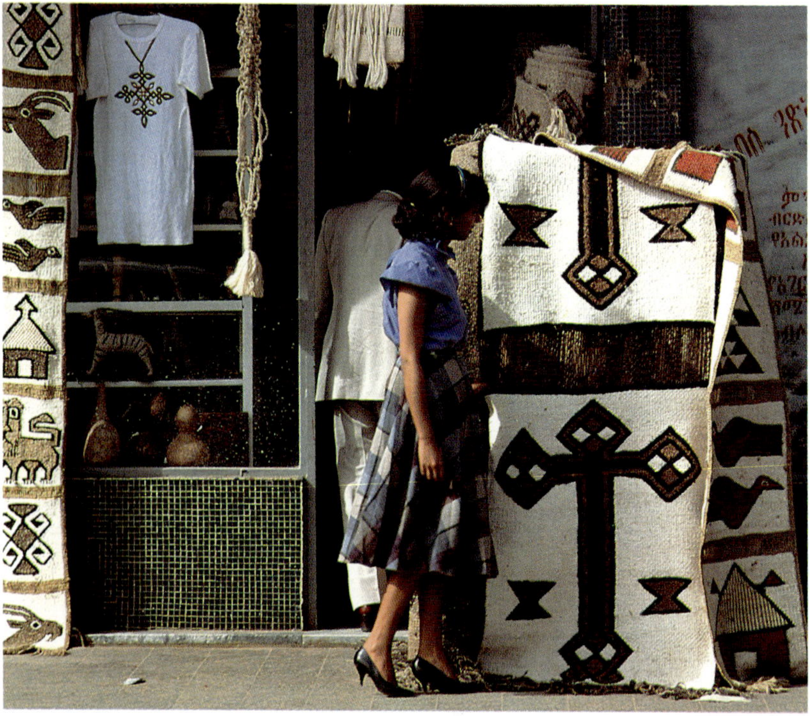

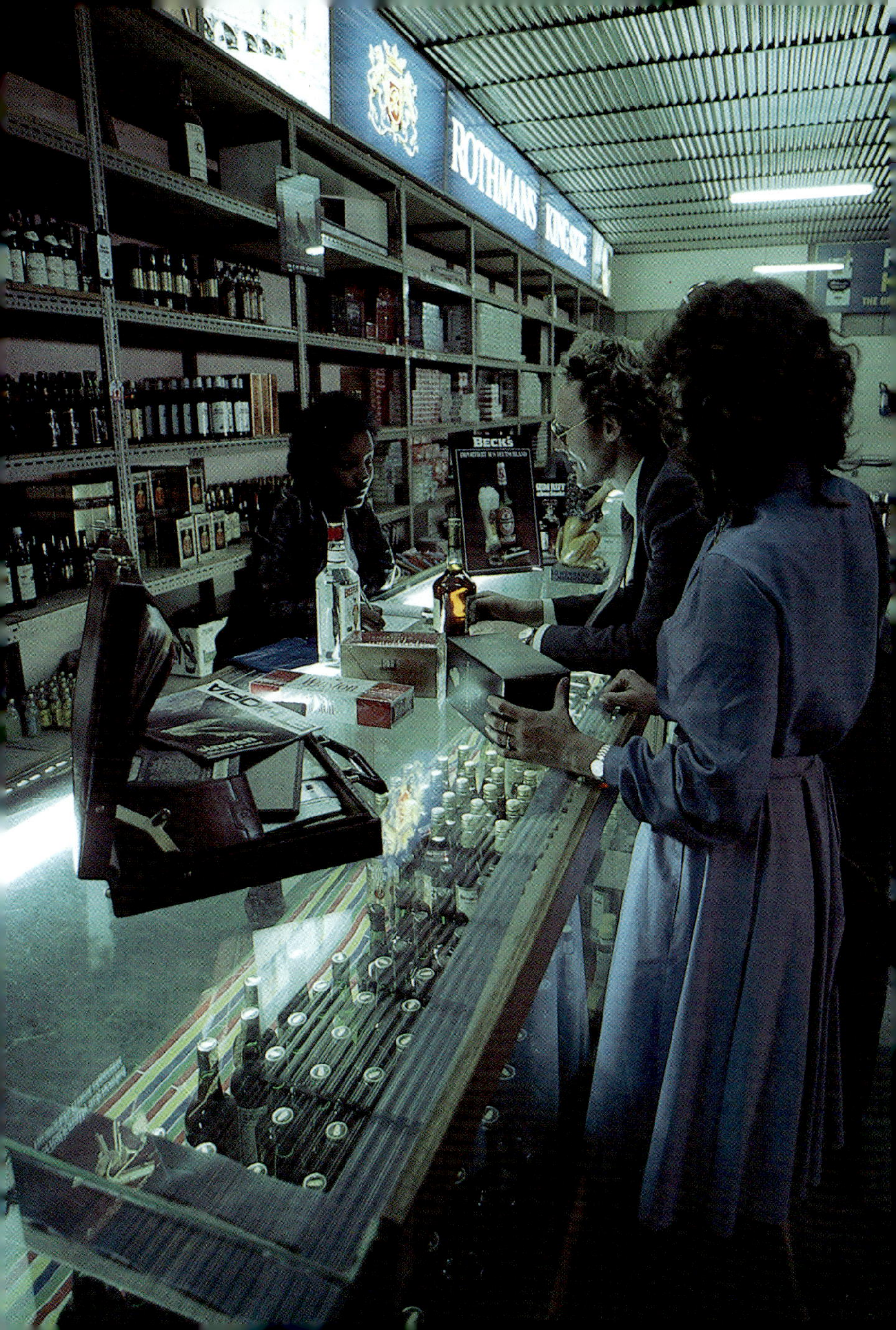
ROTHMANS
KING SIZE
BECK'S

There is a genuine effort under way in all quarters of Ethiopia to make people more mindful of time, but old habits die hard; the person who expects punctuality and a sense of urgency will be unduly frustrated in Ethiopia. Another highland proverb says that "patience is bitter, but her fruits are sweet". Take heed of this bit of wisdom and allow yourself as much time as you can in all your dealings in Ethiopia.

In the highlands and among traditional folk smoking is not appreciated and it is forbidden inside church grounds and in front of priests. Removing your shoes is another courtesy expected of you when entering church buildings or mosques.

Customs Formalities

Besides personal effects, a visitor may import duty-free spirits (including liquors) or wine up to one litre, perfume and toilet water up to half a litre, and 250 grams (half a pound) of tobacco (up to 200 cigarettes or 50 cigars).

If you are carrying a video camera, laptop computer, or any other piece of sophisticated electronic equipment, it is usually entered in your passport to ensure that you take it with you when you go and do not sell it while in the country. You do not need to declare still cameras, small shortwave radios, calculators, and similar small electronic devices. Professional journalists and photographers must report to the Ministry of Information to get a permit.

A permit is given for temporary import of certain items — such as trade samples or professional articles — which must be produced on departure or duty will be paid.

Visitors may import up to Ethiopia birr 10 and an unlimited amount of foreign currency, providing declaration of such currency (on the appropriate blue-coloured form) is made to

Overleaf: A fleet of luxury air-conditioned buses run by the National Tour Operators await visitors outside Addis Ababa's Ghion Hotel.

Customs on arrival. This currency declaration form will be required by Customs on departure.

A permit from the appropriate authorities is required for export of antiques and wildlife products.

All your purchases in Ethiopia can be packed, cleared and dispatched to you by forwarding agents.

Diplomatic Missions and International Organisations

Addis Ababa is Africa's premier diplomatic centre. The Organisation of African Unity (OAU) and the United Nations Economic Commission for Africa (UN-ECA) are headquartered here. There are many diplomatic missions and international organisations in Addis Ababa.

Embassies:

Algeria, tel: 71.13.00/65.23.00	Fax: 65.01.87
Angola, tel: 51.34.56	Fax: 51.00.85
Austria, tel: 71.21.44	Fax: 71.21.40
Belgium, tel: 61.18.13/61.16.43	Fax: 61.36.46
Bulgaria, tel: 61.33.70/61.34.63	
Burundi, tel: 65.28.78/65.13.00	Fax: 65.02.99
Cameroon, tel: 51.48.44/51.46.07	
Canada, tel: 71.30.22/71.30.33	Fax: 71.13.33
Chad, tel: 61.18.19	Fax: 61.20.50
China, tel: 71.19.60	Fax: 71.16.11
Congo, tel: 51.41.88/51.43.31	
Cote d'Ivoire, tel: 71.12.13	Fax: 71.21.78
Cuba, tel: 71.25.25	Fax: 71.03.55
Czech Republic, tel: 51.61.32	Fax: 51.34.71
Djibouti, tel: 61.30.06/61.32.00	Fax: 61.25.04
Egypt, tel: 55.00.21/55.30.77	Fax: 55.27.22

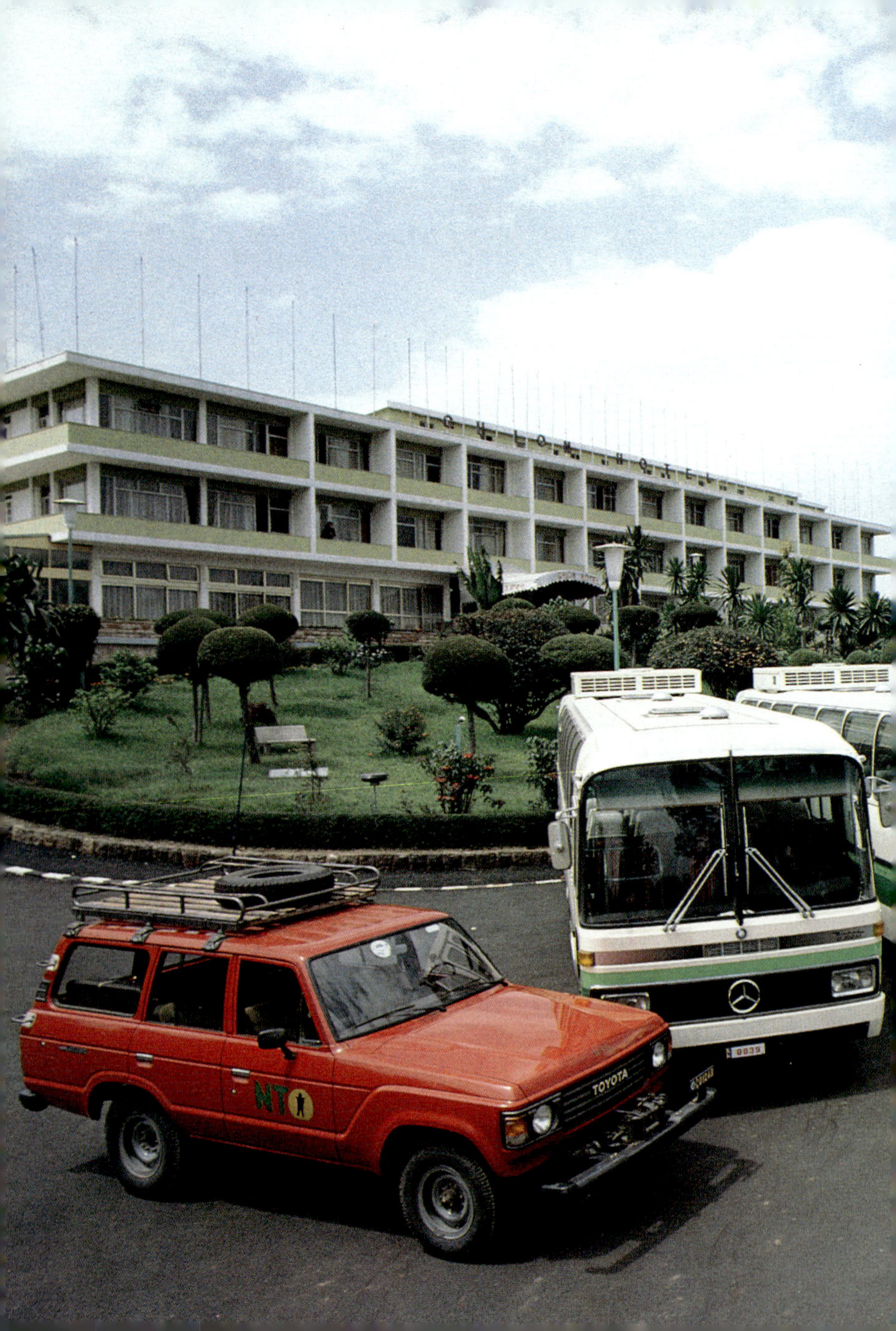
TOYOTA

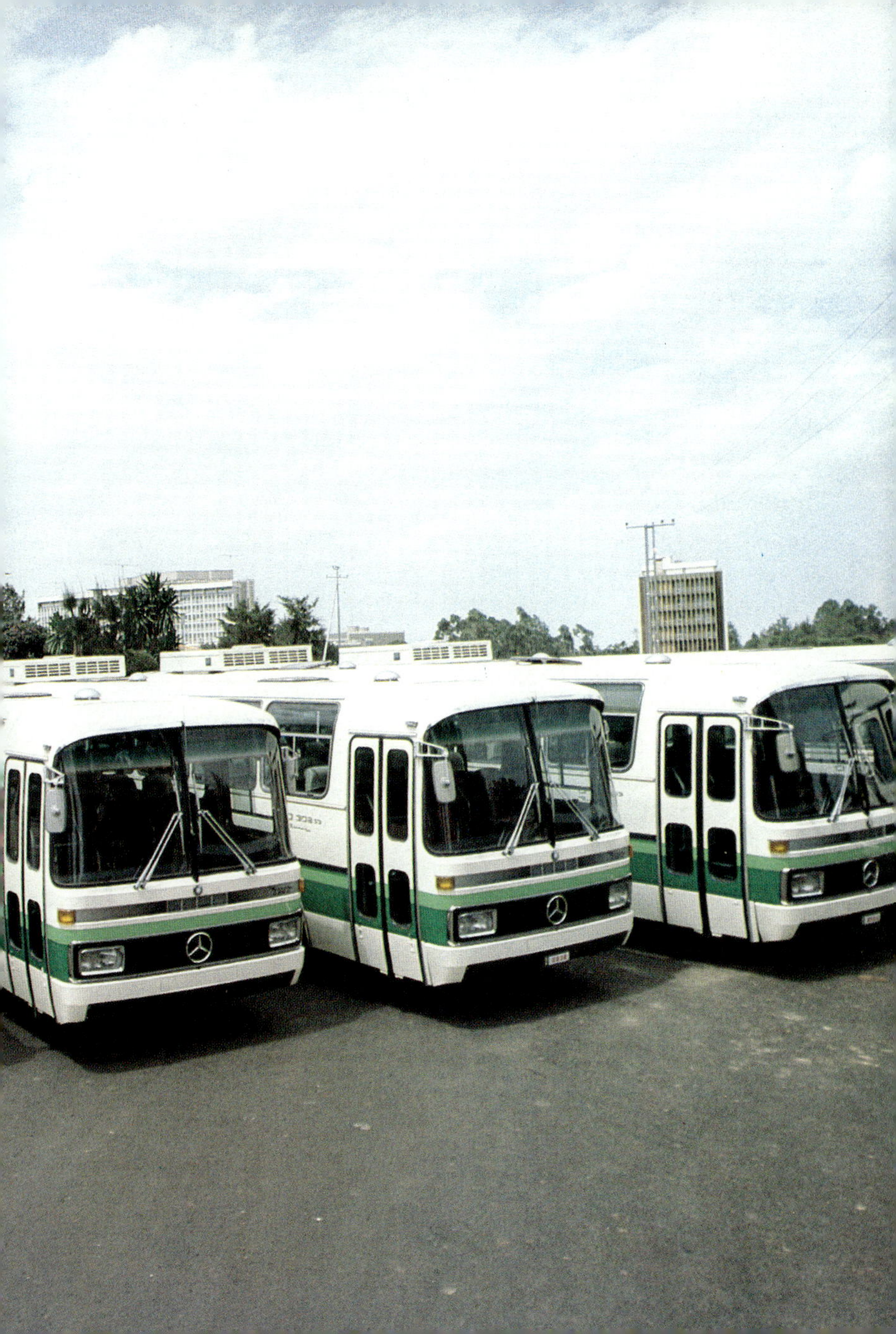

Equatorial Guinea, tel: 61.00.34	
Eritrea, tel: 51.29.40/51.43.02	Fax: 51.49.51
Finland, tel: 51.39.40/51.43.02	Fax: 51.38.54
France, tel: 55.00.66	Fax: 55.11.80
Gabon, tel: 61.10.75	Fax: 61.30.00
Germany, tel: 55.04.33	Fax: 55.13.11
Ghana, tel: 71.14.02	Fax: 71.25.11
Greece, tel: 65.49.12	Fax: 65.48.83
Guinea, tel: 65.12.50/65.13.08	Fax: 65.12.50
Vatican, tel: 71.21.00	Fax: 71.14.99
India, tel: 55.23.94/55.21.00	Fax: 55.25.21
Indonesia, tel: 71.21.04	Fax: 71.08.73
Iran, tel: 71.00.37	Fax: 71.22.99
Ireland, tel: 61.33.61/61.27.71	
Israel, tel: 61.09.99/61.24.56	Fax: 61.06.08
Italy, tel: 55.15.65/55.30.44	Fax: 55.02.18
Japan, tel: 51.10.88	Fax: 51.13.50
Kenya, tel: 61.00.33/61.03.03	Fax: 61.14.33
Korea, Democratic People's tel: 75.00.69	
Korea, Republic of, tel: 71.01.17/71.01.25	Fax: 61.08.61
Liberia, tel: 51.36.55/51.37.91	Fax: 51.13.83
Libya, tel: 51.10.77/51.10.78	Fax: 51.13.83
Madagascar, tel: 61.25.55	Fax: 61.01.27
Malawi, tel: 71.24.40	Fax: 71.04.90
Mozambique, tel: 71.90.56	Fax: 71.00.21
Namibia, tel: 61.19.66	Fax: 61.26.77
Netherlands, tel: 71.11.00	Fax: 71.15.77
Niger, tel: 65.11.75/65.13.05	Fax: 65.12.96
Nigeria, tel: 55.23.06/55.23.08	Fax: 55.23.07
Norway, tel: 71.07.99	Fax: 71.12.55
Palestine, tel: 61.08.11	Fax: 61.11.99

Overleaf: View of the twisting, precipitous road between Dessie and Kombolcha.

Romania, tel: 61.01.56/61.11.91	
Russia, tel: 61.01.56/61.11.91	Fax: 61.37.95
Rwanda, tel: 61.03.00/61.03.57	Fax: 61.04.11
Saudi Arabia, tel: 71.77.99	Fax: 71.77.99
Senegal, tel: 61.13.76	Fax: 61.00.20
Sierra Leone, tel: 71.00.33	Fax: 71.11.19
Spain, tel: 55.02.22	Fax: 55.11.31
Sudan, tel: 51.64.77	Fax: 51.81.41
Sweden, tel: 51.66.99	Fax: 51.58.30
Switzerland, tel: 71.05.77/71.11.07	Fax: 71.21.77
Tanzania, tel: 51.10.63/51.81.55	Fax: 51.73.58
Tunisia, tel: 65.38.18	Fax: 65.02.33
Turkey, tel: 61.23.21	Fax: 61.16.88
Uganda, tel: 51.52.85/51.31.15	Fax: 51.43.55
United Kingdom, tel: 61.23.54	Fax: 61.05.88
USA, tel: 55.10.02/55.06.66	Fax: 55.11.66
Yemen, tel: 71.09.90/71.18.11	Fax: 71.09.91
Yugoslavia, tel: 51.78.04	Fax: 51.67.63
Zaire, tel: 71.01.11/71.01.20	Fax: 71.14.85
Zambia, tel: 71.13.02	Fax: 71.15.66
Zimbabwe, tel: 61.38.77	Fax: 61.34.76

Doctors and Dentists

Medical facilities are limited and of generally poor standard. Existing facilities are sorely overtaxed. Tourists and non-citizen residents should go to private hospitals and clinics or ask your hotel to call a doctor. Your embassy will also be able to refer you to a recommended doctor. If you fall seriously ill you may want to consider evacuation to nearby Nairobi or to Europe. Air rescue services are available, and you might want to make arrangements with one before your trip.

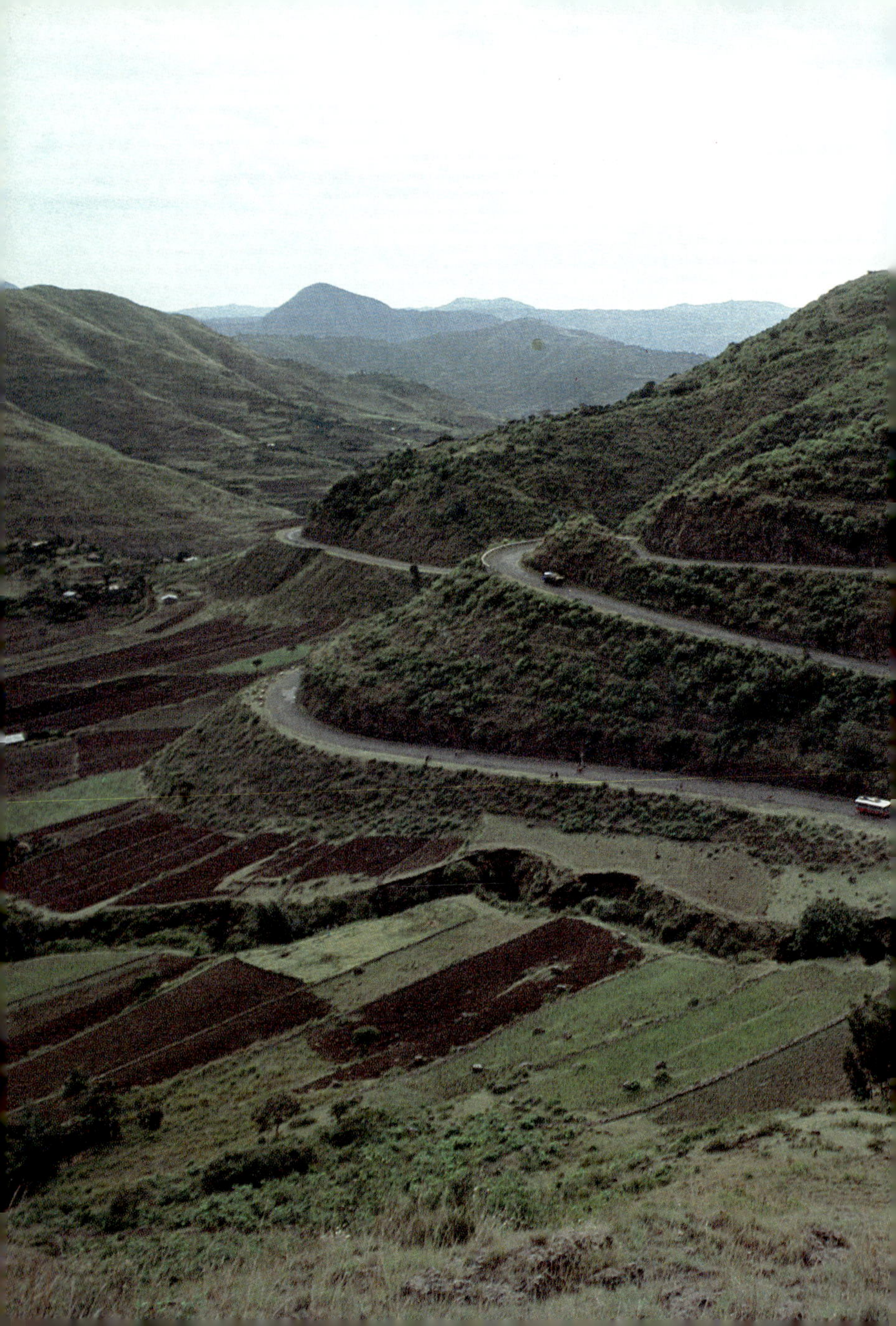

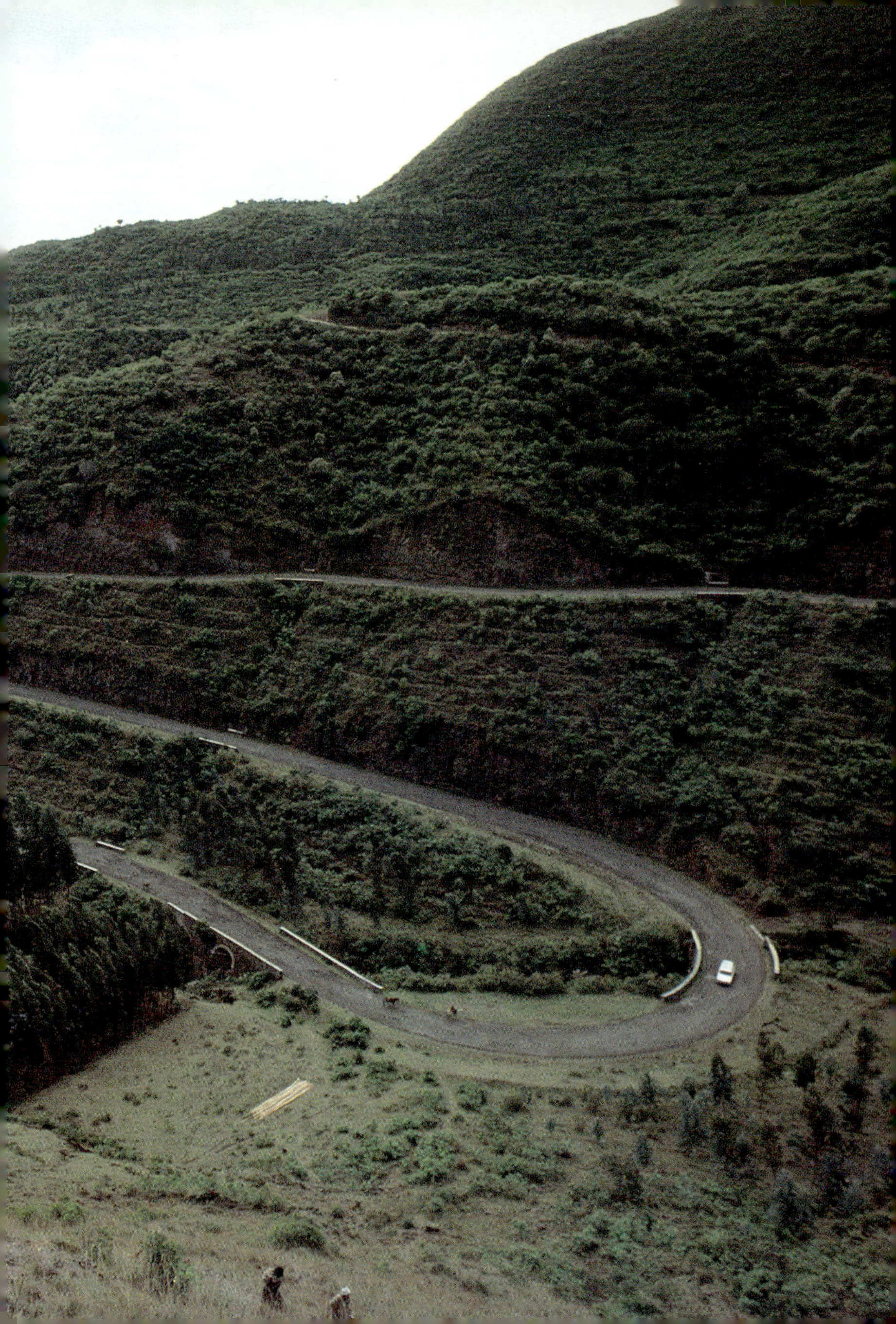

Some hospitals and clinics in Addis Ababa:
ALERT Hospital, Amanuel Hospital, Armed Forces Hospital, Balcha Hospital, Black Lion Hospital, Ethio Swedish Children's Hospital, Fistula Hospital, Ghandi Hospital, Menelik II Hospital, Police Hospital, Ras Desta Hospital, St.Paul Hospital, St.Peter Hospital, Tatek Sene 18 Hospital, Yekatit 12 Hospital, Yemewodesh Maternity Hospital, Zewditu Memorial Hospital.

The hospitals and pharmacies are put on rotation for service during the night and on public holidays. You will find which are on duty from the radio or the daily newspapers.

Electrical Current

Electricity supply is 220 volts 50 cycles AC. American-manufactured electrical appliances usually need an adaptor before they can be plugged into wall sockets. Sudden, unexpected blackouts can happen even in Addis Ababa.

Health and Visa Requirements

All visitors (including infants) are required to possess a valid yellow fever vaccination certificate. Vaccination against cholera is also required for any person who has visited or transited a cholera-infested area within six days prior to arrival in Ethiopia. Your doctor may also recommend gamma globulin shots or refresher vaccines of typhoid and polio before you go. Hepatitis, typhoid, menengitis, and other communicable diseases do exist in the country, but most tourists will run little risk of coming in contact with them.

Visas are required for all visitors to Ethiopia, with the exception of nationals of Djibouti, Eritrea, Kenya, and Sudan. Visas should be applied for well in advance of any trip as applications can take time to process.

Except in the case of a few nationals, passengers in transit in Ethiopia holding confirmed onward bookings within 72 hours can obtain transit visas on arrival for a fee of Ethiopian birr 20. However, in this case, passports are held at the airport until departure and a pink-coloured receipt card is issued.

Health Precautions

Prophylactics against malaria (not in fact necessary in Addis Ababa as the city itself is above the malaria risk zone) are advisable if you have planned trips in the countryside, especially to the lowlands. In the outlying regions it is wise to drink only boiled water, or the bottled mineral waters that are available everywhere. Swimming in lakes or rivers should be avoided, as there is always a risk of contracting bilharzia. However, hotel swimming pools, the many hot-water springs, and the alkaline lakes at Debre Zeit and Langano are safe to swim in.

Travellers should remember that Ethiopia is the 'Roof of Africa', and that the high altitude of most of the country puts a strain on the heart and nervous system until one is acclimatised, so avoid any unnecessary physical exertion for the first few days. Sufferers from heart ailments or high blood pressure should consult their doctor before travelling to Ethiopia. Avoid contact with stray dogs and cats as a precaution against rabies.

Hotels

The Historic Route is served by the largest chain, the Ghion. The east belongs to the Ras, the west to the Ethiopians, and the south to the Wabi Shebelle. The specialised Filwoha chain consists of spas such as Wondo Guenet, and Sodere resort. The Hilton is independently managed.

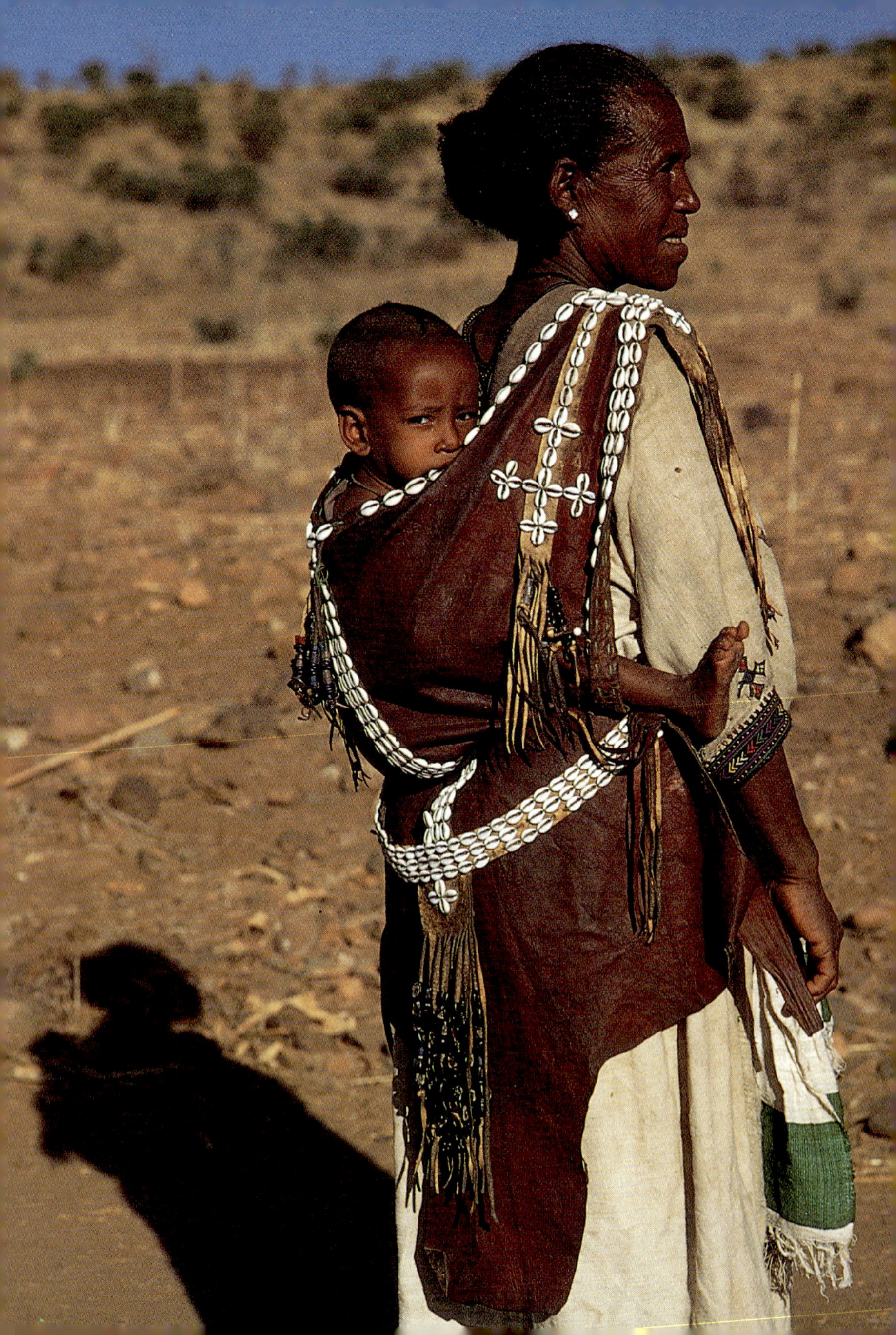

Opposite: Traditional Ethiopian way to carry a baby.

Below: Mursi woman with lip plate.

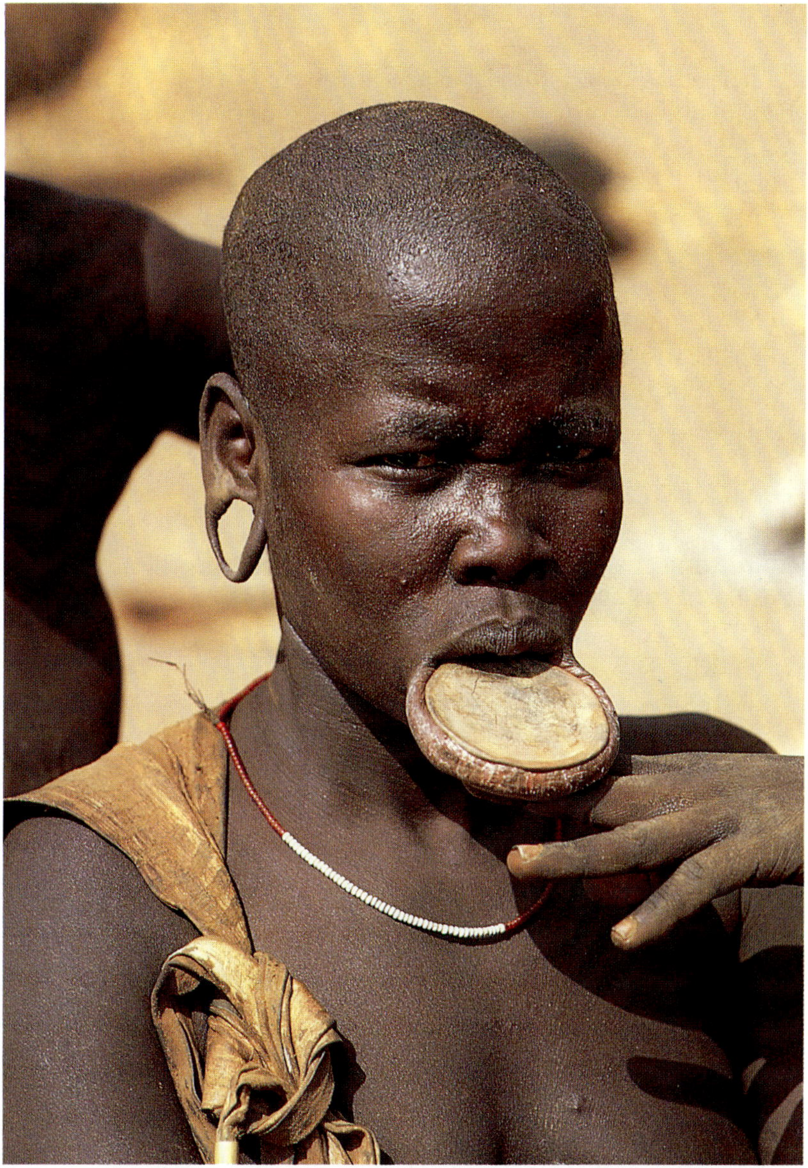

There are good tourist-class hotels in Addis Ababa, along the Historic Route, Harar, Dire Dawa, and the northern Rift Valley Lakes area. Rather spartan accommodation is also available in all the major towns, but these hotels and lodging houses are not recommended for tourists, unless absolutely necessary.

The Addis Ababa Hilton International is, of course, a luxury hotel of international standard. The nearby Ghion Hotel makes a good, and slightly less expensive, alternative. The 295 room Addis Sheraton has recently opened, with excellent service, food, accommodation and amenieties.

Hotels in Addis Ababa include

Hilton International
PO Box 1164
tel: 51.84.00
telex: 21204
fax: 51.00.64

Sheraton Hotel
(Opening 1997)

Ethiopia Hotel
PO Box 1131
tel: 51.74.00
telex: 21072

Harambee Hotel
PO Box 3340
tel: 51.40.00/51.44.82
telegram: HARAMBE

Ghion Hotel
PO Box 1643
tel: 51.32.22
telex: 21112
fax: 51.53.81

Airport Motel
PO Box 100520
Tel: 61.04.22
telex: 21700
Fax: 61.05.77

Overleaf: The sixteenth-century Susneyos Palace near Gorgora served as a model for the famous Gondar palaces.

Wabe Shebelle Hotel
PO Box 3154
tel: 51.71.87
telegram: WABSHO
telex: 21416 WASO ET

Ras Hotel,
PO Box 1632
tel: 51.70.60/51.70.63
telex: 21485

Ambo: Ambo Hotel
Arba Minch: Bekele Mola Hotel
Asela: Asela Ras Hotel
Awasa: Awasa Hotel I, Awasa Hotel II
Awash National Park: Kereyu Lodge
Axum: Axum Hotel, Ezana Hotel, Kaleb Hotel, Yoha Hotel
Bahar Dar: Bahar Dar Ghion Hotel; Tana Hotel
Debre Zeit: Bekele Mola Hotel, Hora Ras Hotel
Dessie: Ambassel Hotel
Dire Dawa: Kara Mara Ras Hotel; Dier Dawa Ras Hotel
Gambella: Gambella Hotel
Gishen: Gishen Hotel
Goba: Bale Goba ras Hotel
Gondar: Fogera Hotel; Goha Hotel; Quarra Hotel; Terara Hotel
Harar: HararRas Hotel
Jimma: Ghibe Hotel; Gojeb Hotel; Jimma Ethiopia Hotel
Lalibela: Roha Hotel, Seven Olives Hotel
Langano: Langano Hotel; Bekele Mola Hotel
Makale: Abraha Atsbaha Hotel; Adulis Hotel; Green Hotel
Meki: Bekele Mola Hotel
Moyale: Bekele Mola Hotel
Nazaret: Adams Ras Hotel; Bekele Mola Hotel
Robe: Bekele Mola Hotel
Shashemene: Bekele Mola Hotel
Sodere: Sodere Resort Hotel

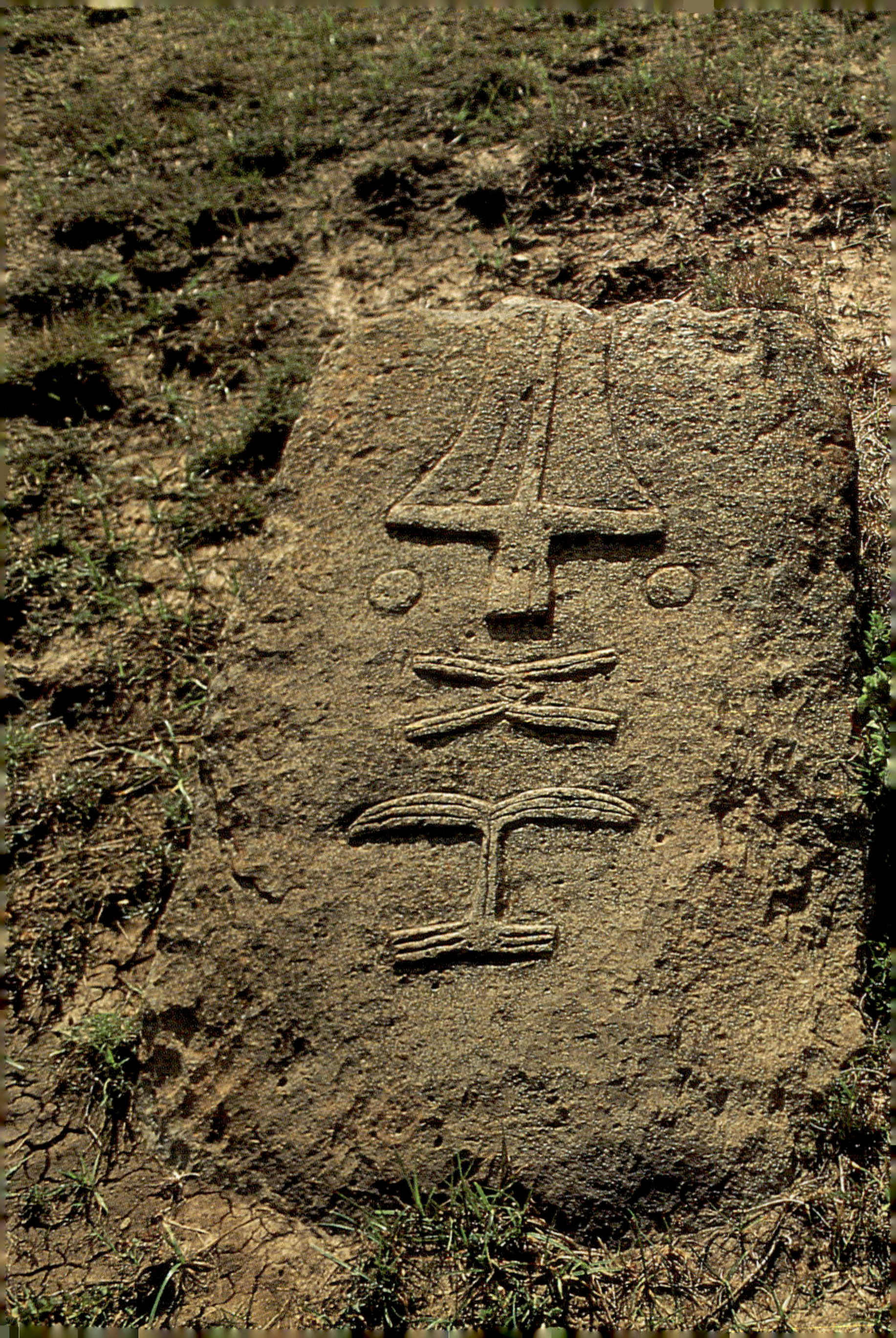

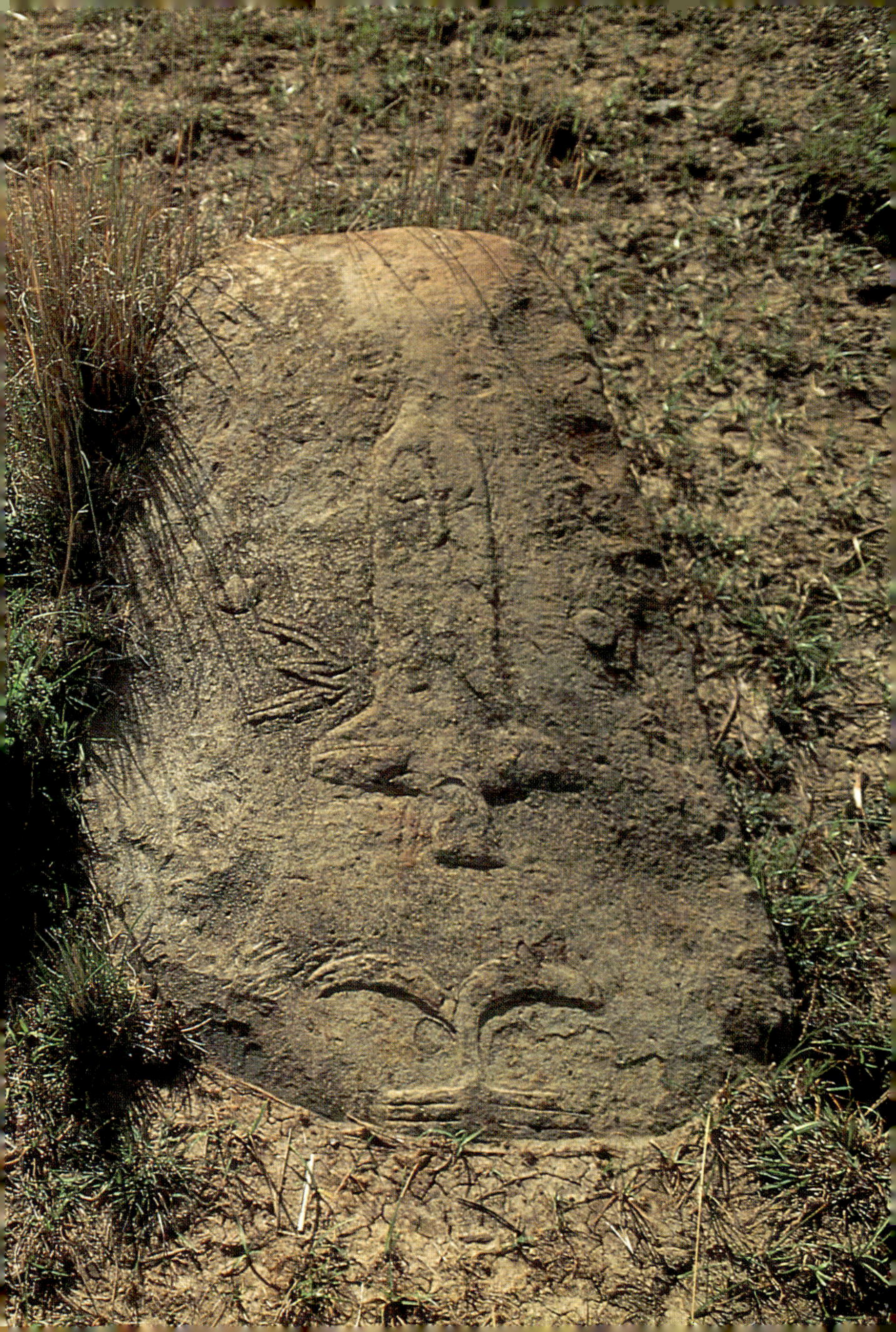

Sodo: Bekele Mola Hotel
Welega: Welega Hotel
Weliso: Weliso Hotel; Walga Hotel
Wendo Guenet: Wendo Guenet Hotel
Ziway: Bekele Mola Hotel

Languages

There are more than 80 major language groups in Ethiopia, but the national language, Amharic, is spoken throughout the country. Orominya and Tigrinya are other widely used Ethiopian languages. English is the second official language and is understood in all the towns and among the modern and educated sector of the population. French, Italian and Arabic are also widely understood.

It is useful to try to learn some words of Amharic, your efforts in this direction will be appreciated. A few useful phrases:

Tena Yistilign - a common greeting, that can be used with anyone and at all occasions.
Sint naw - How much is it?
Mercato yat naw - Where is the Mercato?
Buna alle - Is there coffee?
Yellem - There is not any.
Ameseginalehu - Thank you.

Money

The monetary unit of Ethiopia is the Ethiopian birr, with a par value of E birr 6.4 to US$1.00. The birr is divided decimally, and coins are circulated in values of 1, 5, 10, 25 and 50 cents. Notes are printed in denominations of 1, 5, 10, 50 and 100 birr.

Under Ethiopian law, only the National Bank of Ethiopia may deal in the exchange of foreign currency. However, the Commercial Bank of Ethiopia, its branches, private banks and some major hotels act as agents for the National Bank in exchanging foreign currency. Receipts must be kept as these will permit reconversion into foreign currency.

There are no restrictions on the amount or kind of foreign currency, traveller's cheques, letters of credit or bank drafts which may be imported into Ethiopia by visitors. All currency imported must be declared on the official currency form when entering the country. No Ethiopian currency in excess of E birr 10 may be brought in or taken out of the country by any individual.

Visitors may not export foreign currency in excess of the amount and kind originally brought in. Tourists are expected to have spent a minimum of $50 per day while in the country and this is taken into account when reconverting local currency. Currency may not be exported by mail, except by permission of the National Bank of Ethiopia.

Credit Cards

Some credit cards are accepted in the major hotels and some of the larger restaurants. American Express is the most widely accepted. The Hilton and Ghion hotels also accept Visa, MasterCard and Access. Credit cards are accepted by Ethiopian Airlines and other major carriers.

Nightlife

The Dahlak Paradise (in the same building as the Ambassador Theatre and the Harambee Hotel) was once billed as the most modern and trendy nightclub in Africa, but there are now others to rival its attractions.

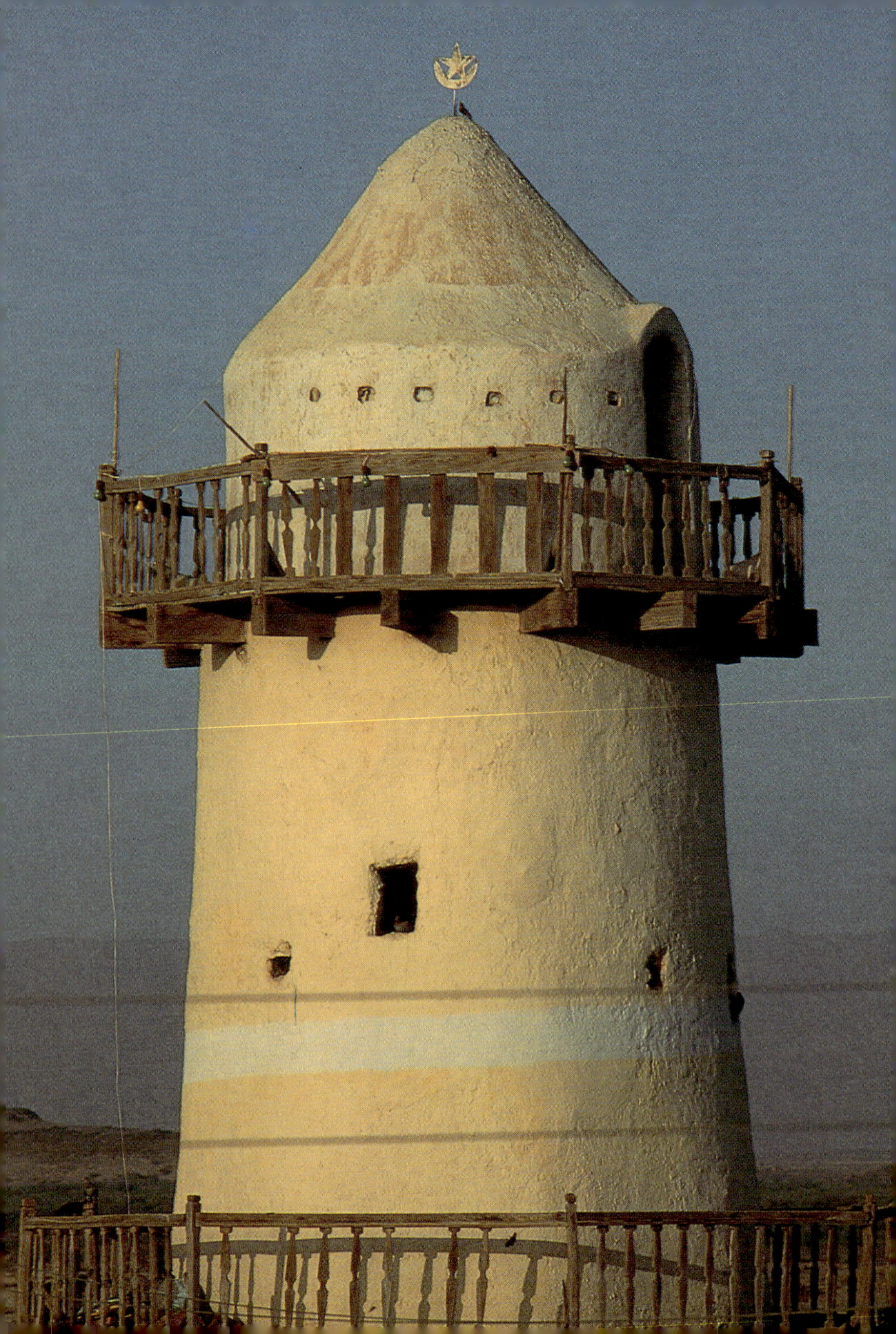

Opposite: Minaret of the Asaita mosque.

Below: Girl carrying gourds near Adwa.

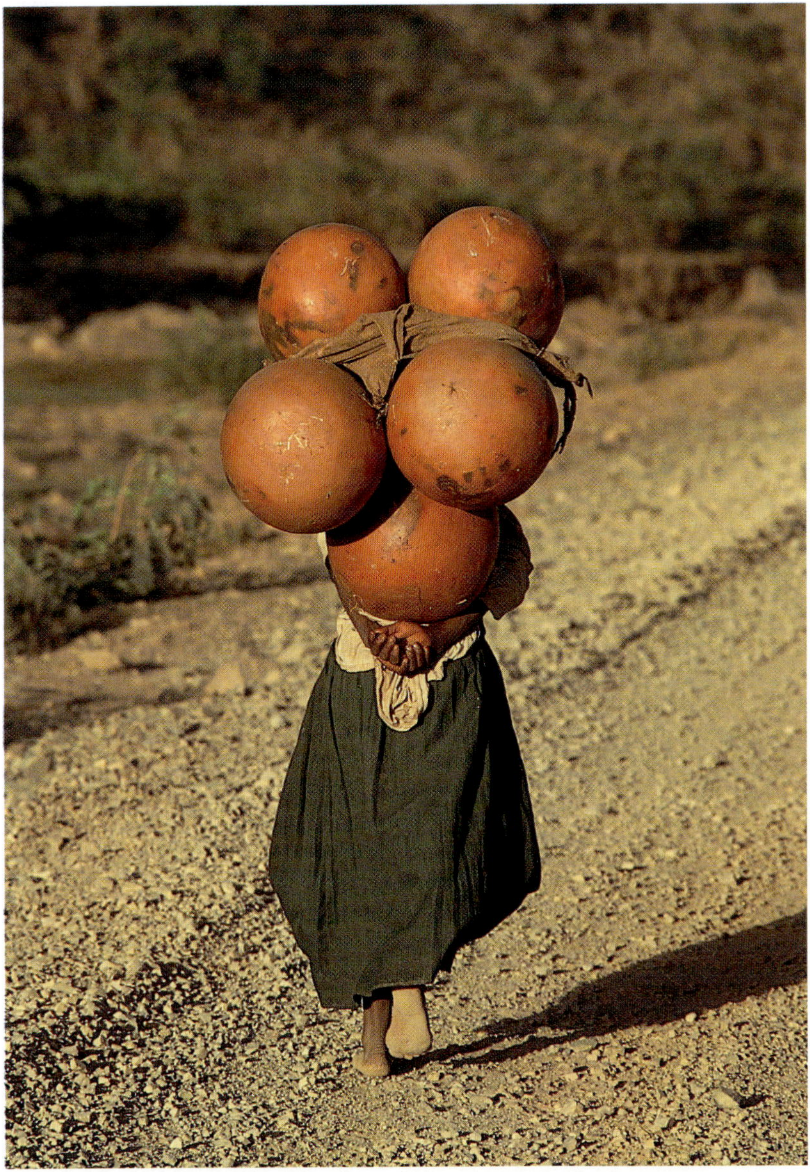

The Ghion Hotel's bar and restaurant, Unity House, is in the best tradition of the hotel. The Africa, Hilton, Ras, and Wabi Shebelle, and many other hotels have nightclubs.

In Ethiopia, a bar is euphemistically called *buna bet* (coffee house). There are many genuine coffee houses, including the excellent and appropriately-named 'Coffee House' (opposite the Egyptian Embassy, near Sidist Kilo). These all offer a friendly atmosphere and some feature traditional folk music.

Pharmacies and pharmaceuticals

Medical supplies are limited in Ethiopia. Visitors should carry an adequate supply of all medicines they may need with them. Those wearing glasses should carry an extra pair — just in case — or, failing that, a prescription. Most chemists and pharmacies maintain regular business hours. Most are open all day on Saturday and there is a system of 'on-duty' pharmacists open to 22.30 or 23.00 and Sundays.

Photography

Most kinds of photographic equipment and films are available only in the duty-free shops in Ethiopia. Visitors are advised to arrive with their own supplies.

Professionals (journalists and travel writers, researchers, etc.) need explicit photographic permits obtained from the Ministry of Infomation. The ordinary tourist does not need such a permit, but it is necessary to proceed with discretion. You should avoid taking photographs of military establishments and strategic installations (and bridges are considered such), and certain Government buildings and Party Headquarters.

Remember that many local people, especially those of the lowlands, are not used to being photographed, and you can arouse their hostility by attempting to take pictures of even their cattle or homes. Muslim women, in particular, have a strong religious objection to being photographed. It is only common sense to be courteous and show reverence in churches and at religious festivals. People usually do not mind a photo taken, although in rural areas frequented by tourists, it is customary to pay for these 'photo opportunities'. It is best to negotiate such arrangements before you click the shutter. If you offend someone, simply but earnestly apologize. Nothing else.

Places of Worship
Most Ethiopians belong to the Ethiopian Orthodox Church or are followers of Islam. Churches and mosques are found throughout the country. On non-fasting days (every Wednesday and Friday being among the 239 fasting days) Orthodox Church services start very early, at 0500.

Muslims observe the five daily hours of *salat* (prayer) and in Addis Ababa *Jummah* is observed at the big Anwar Mosque and other mosques, Fridays at 1200.

The big, modern Trinity Cathedral at Arat Kilo, behind the Old Parliament building, is a good place for attending Orthodox services. Ecumenical services are also occasionally held there.

In Addis Ababa there are places of worship to accommodate most religious creeds.

Armenian Orthodox: St George Church, on Adua Avenue, near Ras Mekonnen Bridge.

Greek Orthodox: St Frumentius Church, on Adua Avenue, at the Piazza Synagogue.

Shalom Shelemy: in Benin Sefer, near Abuna Petros Square

Protestant: **Bethel Church (Presbyterian)**: on Patriots' Street.

Below: The Bale Mountains area is a remarkable world of its own

Opposite: The beautiful Desert Rose.

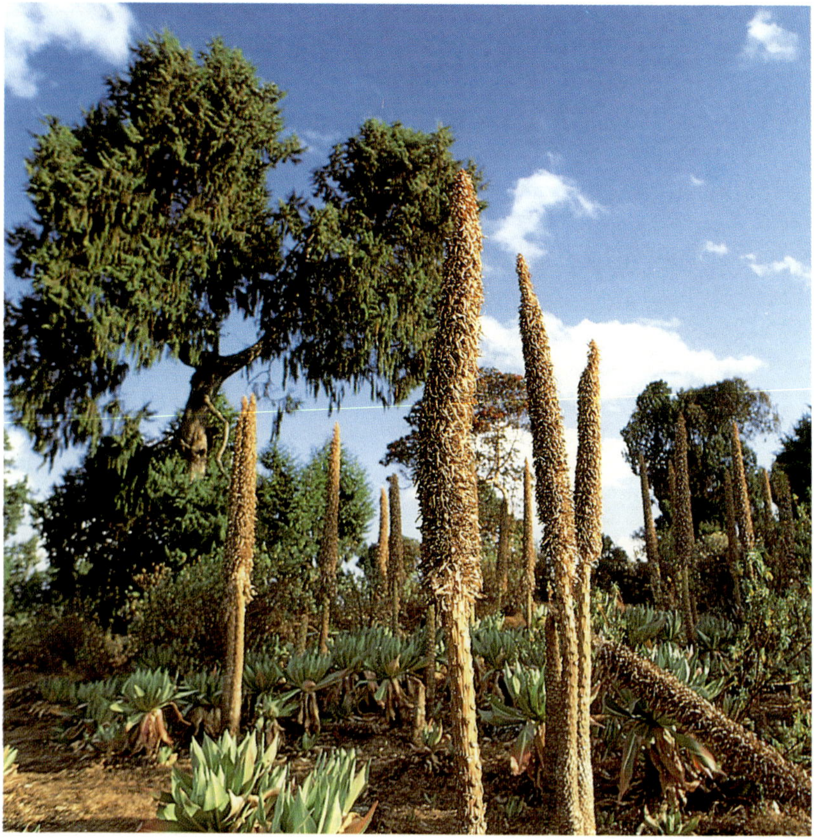

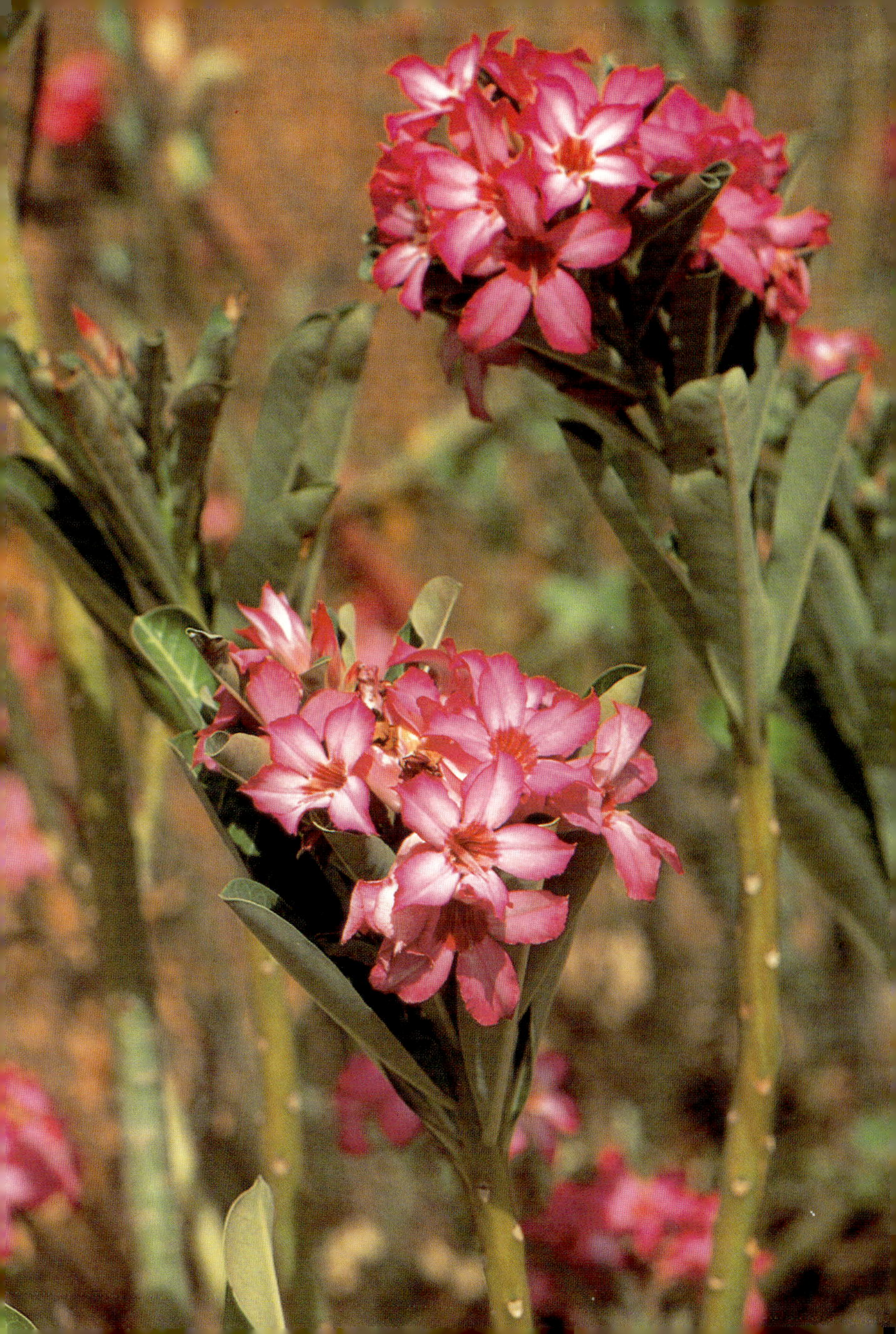

German Congregation of Evangelical Christians: on Omedla Street, at Jan Hoy Meda, near Sidist Kilo.
International Lutheran Church: behind Mitchell Cotts, near Mexico Square.
St Matthew Anglican (Church of England): on the Dessie Road near the YMCA.
Seventh Day Adventist Mission: on Ras Damtew Avenue opposite the Gandhi Memorial Hospital.
Sudan Interior Mission Chapel: opposite the north entrance of Black Lion Hospital.
Roman Catholic: Catholic Cathedral, off Wavel Street, south of the Piazza.
Church of the Holy Saviour: on Churchill Road, below the Ras Hotel
St Gabriel: on Patriots' Street, near Ras Desta Hospital.
St Mary: between the English School and Menilek II Hospital.

Public Holidays

Ethiopia's Sabbath is Sunday. For purposes of observing religious ceremonies and celebration, the Ethiopian Orthodox Church and Ethiopian Islam have many holy days throughout the year, and every church has at least one feast day a month. The following are national public holidays:

7 January	- Ethiopian Christmas *(Gena)*
19 January	- Ethiopian Epiphany *(Timket)*
2 March	- Adwa Day
variable	- Id al Fitr *(Ramadan)*
variable	- Id al Adha *(Arafa)*
1 May	- International Labour Day
variable	- Ethiopian Easter *(Fasika)*
11 September	- Ethiopian New Year's Day *(Engutatash)*

Overleaf: Prehistoric monoliths at Tiya, listed as a World Heritage Site.

27 September - The Finding of the True Cross *(Meskal)*

NB Ethiopian Easter (like European Easter) and the Muslim holidays are based on the lunar calendar and their dates vary from year to year. Office hours of Government establishments, and of most private companies, are from 08.30 to 12.30 and 13.30 to 17.30 Monday through Thursday, and from 08.30 to 11.30 and 13.30 to 17.30 on Friday. Government offices are closed on public holidays, Saturdays and Sundays.

Rail

There is one rail line in Ethiopia. A large proportion of Ethiopia's import-export trade is carried over the 778-kilometre-long Addis Ababa-Djibouti railroad. The line runs through the Awash National Park and across the Rift Valley, traversing the lands of the Afar and Kotu peoples. A train ride from Addis is thus certainly worthwhile if one can bear a day-long ride with few modern conveniences. There are both morning and night trains from both cities, and the journey takes at least 10 hours.

Ethio-Djibouti Railway,
PO Box 1051, Addis Ababa
tel: 51.72.50; telex: 21414

Restaurants

In the top hotels the menus are of international standard. But Addis Ababa also has a number of good restaurants serving Chinese, Italian, French, Greek, Indian and Middle Eastern food.

Ethiopia's main dish is called *wot,* which may be meat or

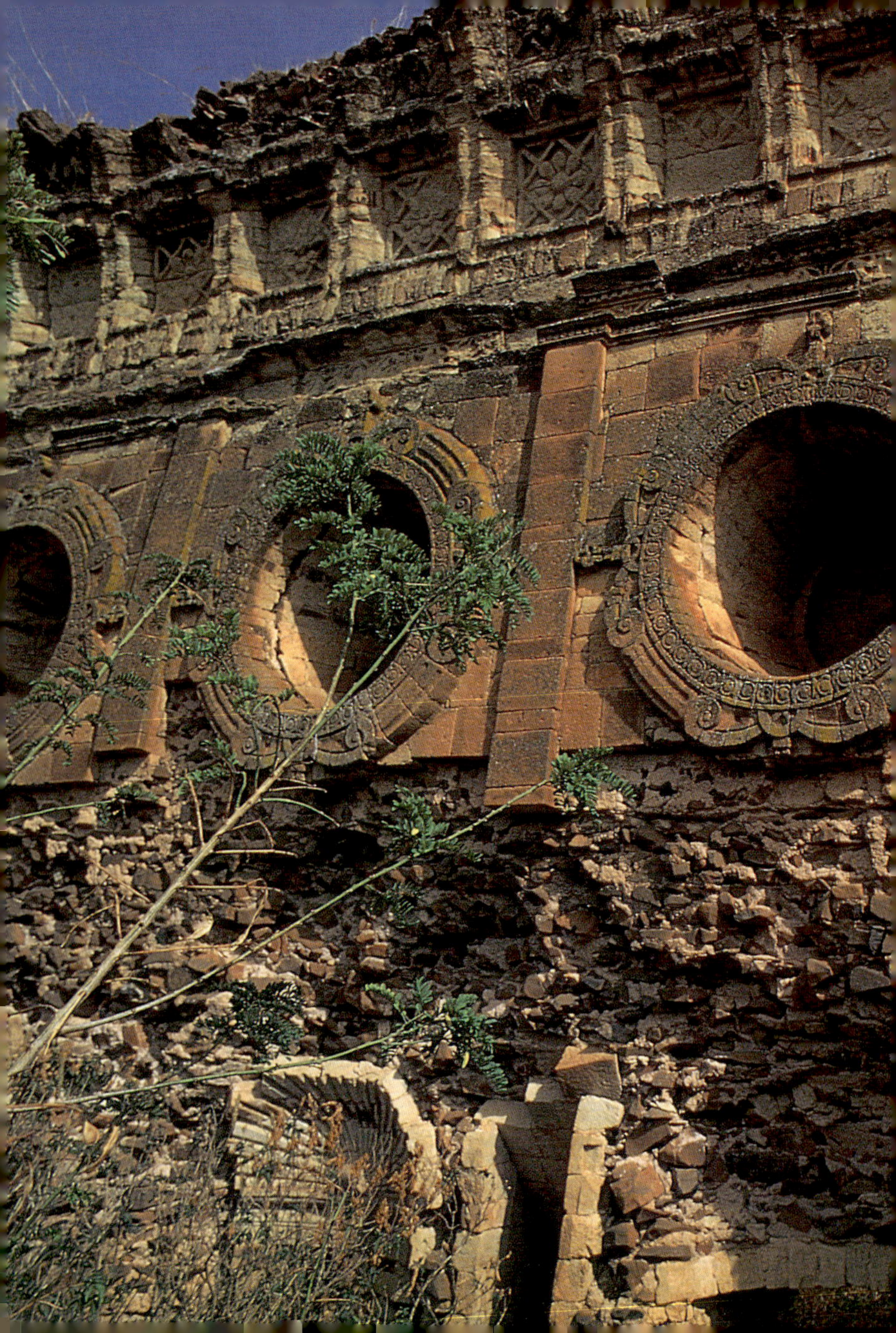

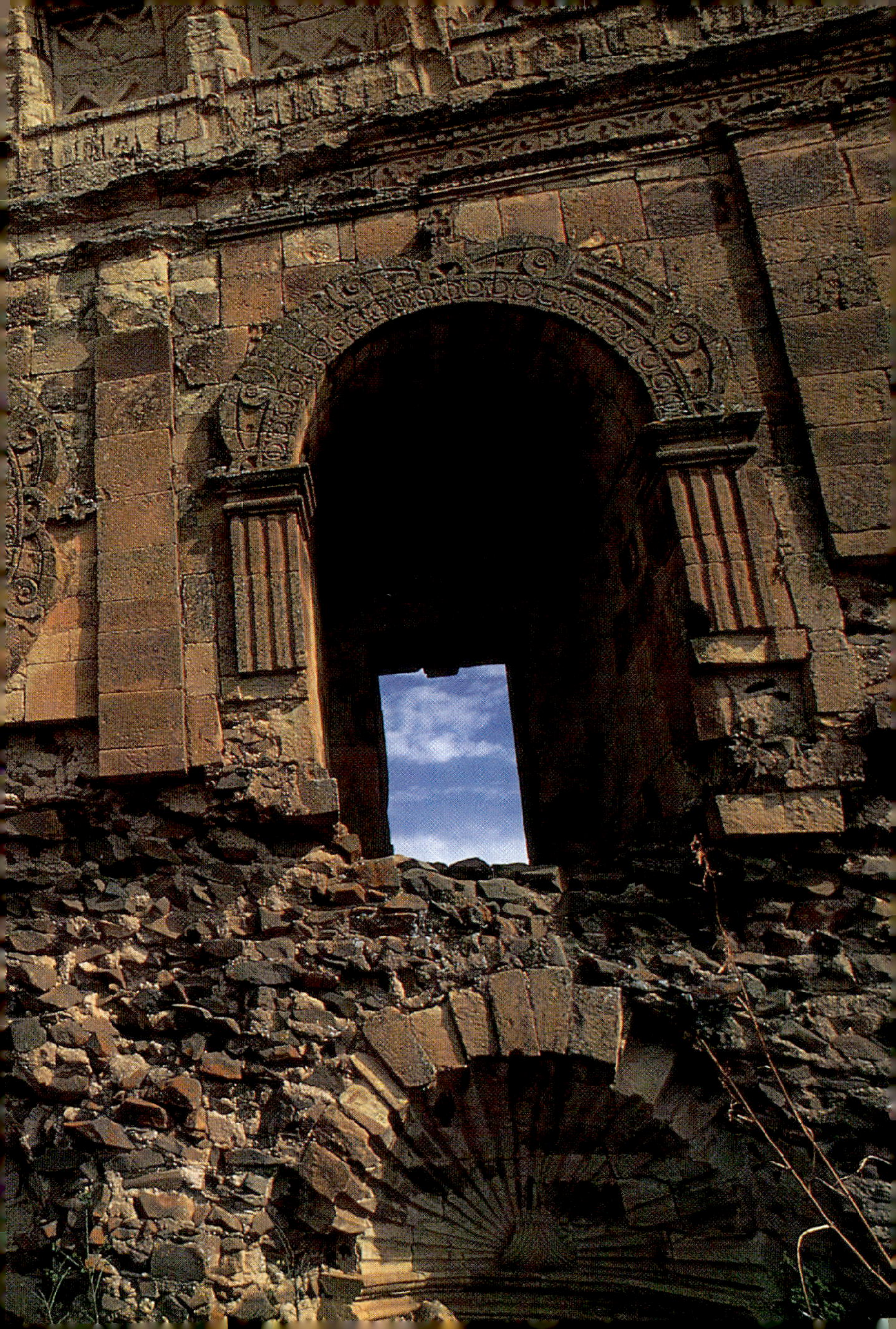

vegetables cooked in a hot, spicy sauce. This is eaten with — and traditionally upon — a flat, spongy bread called *injera.* While chicken *(doro)* wot is probably the single most typical Ethiopian dish, a full meal will generally consist of a number of different dishes. More simple Ethiopian meals may be purchased very cheaply at bars and small local restaurants in all parts of the country.

Tipping

Tips up to ten per cent are an accepted practice and appreciated. At night, tipping the guard who is watching your car outside a restaurant, usually with one birr, is common practice. During the day, street parking boys will want a tip for watching your car while you shop. You are not required to tip them for their unsolicited services, but you may, if you wish to do so. You are not expected to tip a taxi driver on a standard route, just as you would not tip a bus driver. But you can tip the driver of a negotiated trip if the service has been good. In this case a tip of ten per cent is considered generous.

Roads

Northern Ethiopia once had one of the best highway systems in East Africa. Some of these roads — for example the route between Addis Ababa and Dessie — are engineering marvels climbing and descending precipitous gradients through tunnels and hairpin bends, and offer dramatic scenery and panoramic views. The Moyale highway connecting Addis Ababa with Nairobi was completed long ago on the Ethiopian side. Dry weather roads link Addis Ababa also with Djibouti, Khartoum and Hargeisa, in Somalia.

However, road surfaces have deteriorated in recent years and

Overleaf: Vendors come on board to sell refreshments to passengers on the Addis Ababa-Djibouti railway.

travellers should enquire about conditions before embarking on any journey.

All Ethiopian regional capitals are connected by road to Addis Ababa. More than 12,000 kilometres of all-weather roads branch out from the hub of the country to remote and far-flung regions. Of these, some 4,000 kilometres, are fully asphalted, the remainder having gravel surfaces. The 835 kilometre-long highway from Addis Ababa to the Eritrean port of Assab, was completed in 1973. Buses leave daily from Addis Ababa to all the regional capitals and major towns; and all rural points with roads are serviced by buses and micro-buses.

Boats

Ambatch boats, which resemble those depicted in ancient Egyptian tomb murals (built of peeled logs lashed together with bark) are the glory of some of the Rift Valley lakes and are said to be the most handsome still in use anywhere in Africa. Then there are the *tankwas* made of papyrus of Lake Tana, and the hollowed-out tree trunk canoes seen on the Baro and Omo rivers of the south-west. Taking a ride on these simple craft is a memorable experience. There are also modern motorboats available at some of these lakes and rivers.

Shopping

Shopping in Ethiopia can be an exciting activity — if, that is, you are not intimidated by the age-old custom and art of bargaining. Everyone has their own style and approach to a bargaining market; some use simple rules like offering half (or some other fraction) of the price quoted, or pretending not to like prospective purchases in order to elicit a more reasonable price. Another way is simply to decide how much

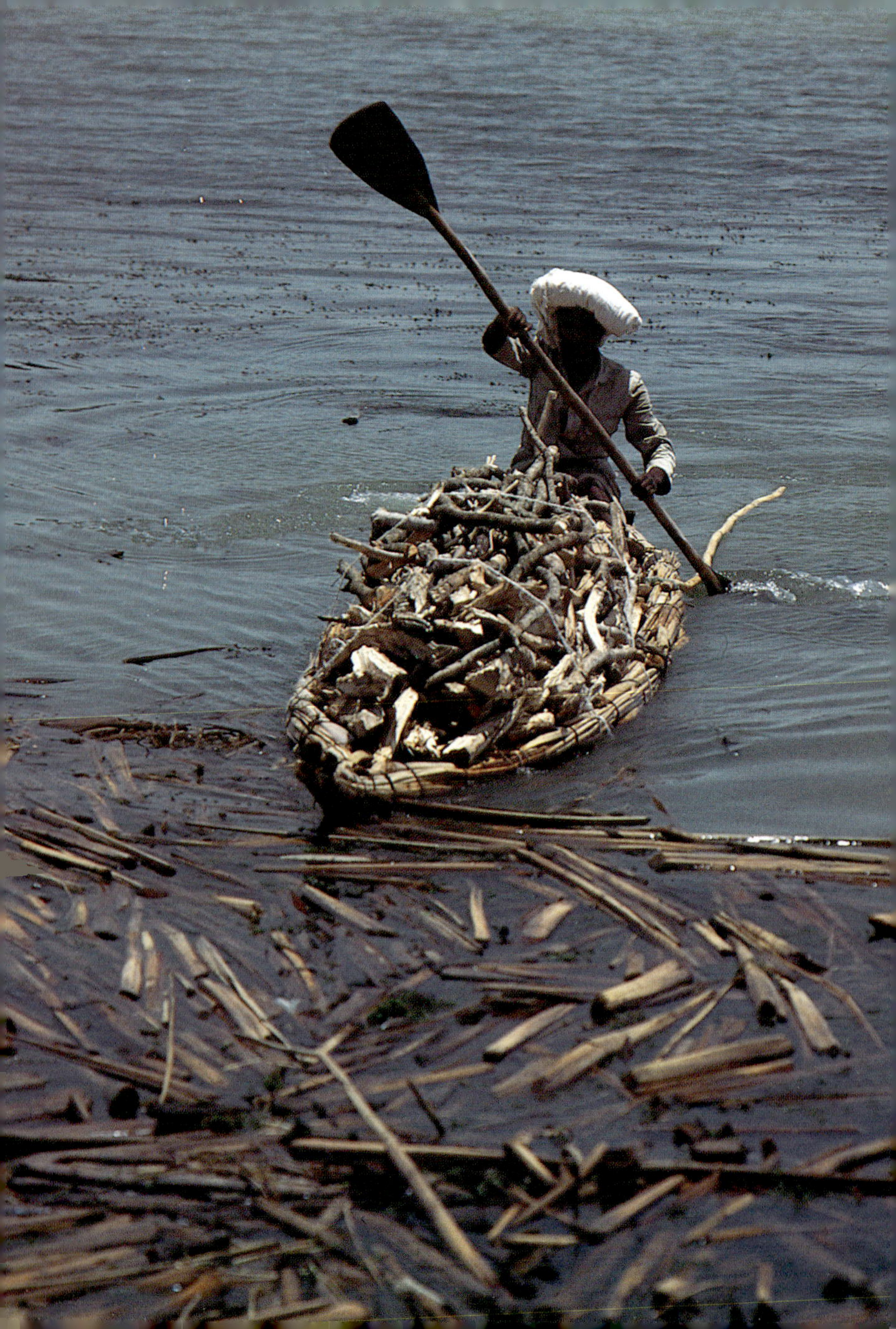

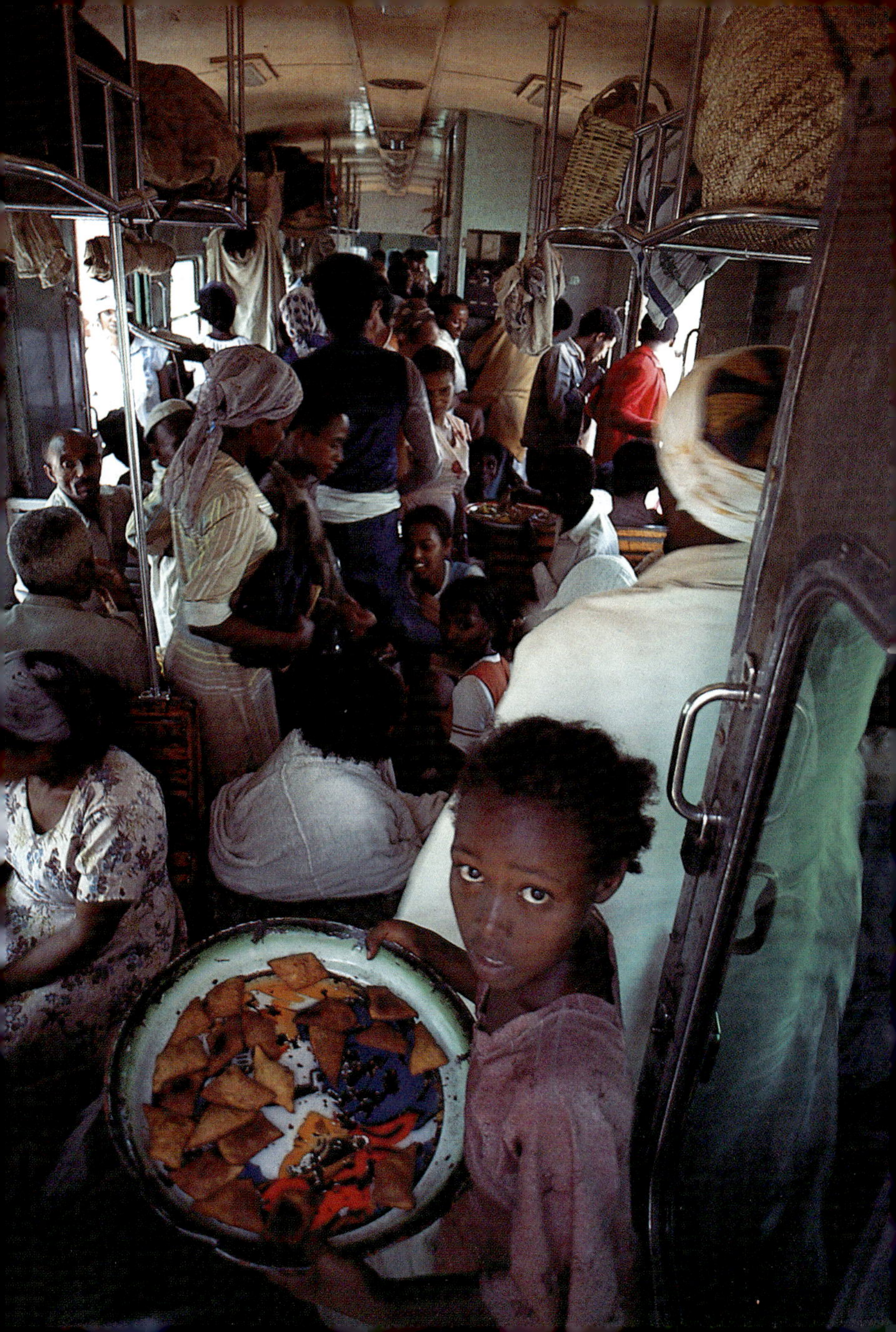

Previous page: Papyrus boats are still used to ferry firewood on Lake Tana.

you are willing to pay for an item and make that your counter-offer. However, you should not then feel that you have been cheated if the item you are after is readily delivered to you at that price.

Shopping in the Mercato, Africa's largest open-air market, is fun, and attractive bargains are plentiful. Here you will find the colourful basket work and silver filigree of Harar, the three-legged stools of Jimma, the hand-made wool carpets of Debre Birhan, the crosses of Gondar, along with the pottery, wood carving, embroidered cloth, parchments and jewellery of all the different regions of Ethiopia.

Animal products such as skins, and antiques deemed to be relics, require export clearance. The Wildlife Conservation Authority and the Antiquities Authority will provide this.

The Ethio-Craft Rehabilitation Centre on the Dessie Road, and the Handicrafts and Small Industries Development Agency (opposite the Wabi Shebelle Hotel) sell gorgeous rugs, amongst other things. Ethio-Craft also has an outlet shop, 'The Ark' at the Piazza.

The following are some of the recommended shops for national costumes, animal skins and a variety of souvenirs:
ETTC Gift Shop, Piazza
Jolly Gift Articles
Meridian, near OAU
Wabi Shebele Gift Shop

For gold and silver jewellery:
Asgedom Gessesse Gold and Silversmith
Ghermay Kidane Jewellers
Haile S Alemayehu Jewellers

Johar Mohammed
Pizant Nabandian
Tana Jewellers
Teclu Desta

Groceries and supermarkets in Addis Ababa include:
Abadir Groceries
Asfaw Tekle Grocery
Dagmawe Grocery
Fanta Supermarket
Harambee Grocery
Misrak Supermarket
Nile Grocery
Showa Grocery

Telecommunications and the Postal Service

The Sululta satellite earth station, linked to the INTELSAT Atlantic Ocean satellite in 1974, has boosted Ethiopia's modern telecommunications capacity, with the result that direct telephone links are now enjoyed with many countries. Nationally, trunk dialling systems exist between Addis Ababa and Awasa, Bahar Dar, Debre Zeit, Dessie, Dire Dawa, Gondar, Harar, Jimma, Makale, and Shashamene. Telegram offices in Addis Ababa are open around the clock. There are telex facilities at the Hilton and bigger hotels and telephone facilities for the press at the Telecommunications Centre near the Ras Hotel.

Time

GMT + 3. This is true but misleading since Ethiopia not only has its own calendar of 13 months, but it also reckons the hours of the day differently. You must keep this in mind when

Opposite: Huge termite mound in southern Ethiopia.

making or accepting appointments. When an Ethiopian says he will meet you at eight, he may mean at 1400.

Ethiopian time goes by 12-hour cycles of day and night. One cycle starts with 'one' at 0700 and goes on to 'twelve' which is 1800; another cycle starts at 1900 ('one' again) and goes through to 0600 ('twelve'). And while in Ethiopia, where the Julian calendar is in force, remember that you are seven years, eight months and at least a week younger, always.

Tour companies

Caravan Travel & Tour Agency,
Tel 516501, 158370 , 122651 (24 hrs); Fax 553656

Experience Ethiopia Travel
Tel 152336, 519291; Fax 519982

Four Seasons Travel & Tour Trading PLC,
Tel 613121, 613616; Fax 513183

National Tour Operation (NTO)
Tel 513383, 512955; Fax 517688

Travel Ethiopia
Tel 150036, 553767; Fax 551276, 510200

Yumo Tours
Tel 518878; Fax 513451

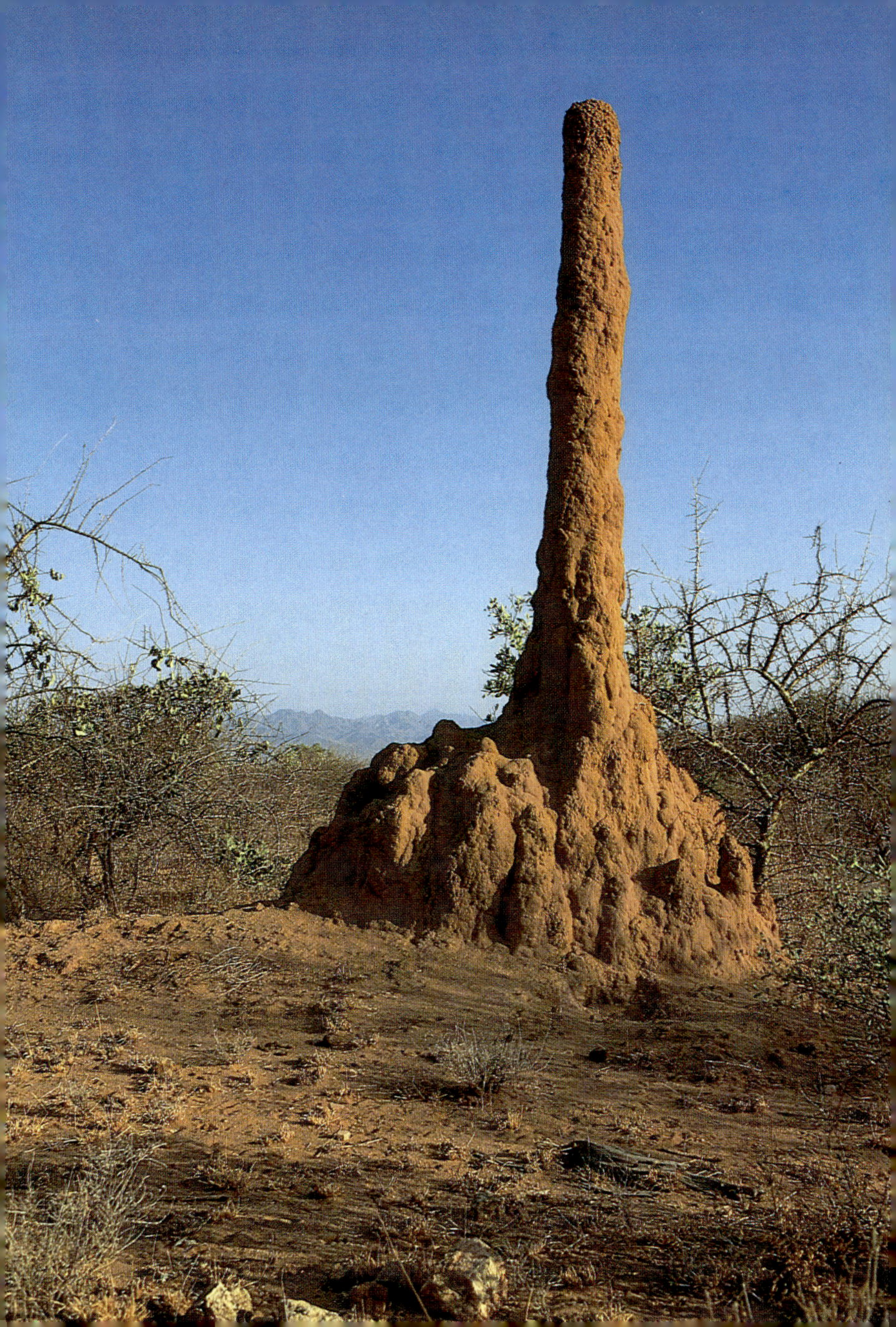

Daylight

Being relatively close to the equator, there is an almost constant twelve hours of daylight. In Addis Ababa, the sunrise and sunset start at around 06.30 and 18.45 respectively.

What to Wear

In lowland areas the lightest possible cotton clothing, with a hat and sunglasses, is all that is required. In Addis Ababa and throughout the highlands, where the climate is more like that of spring in the Mediterranean, or a good early summer in northern Europe, light to medium-weight clothing is appropriate. During the rainy season, from June through September, an umbrella or raincoat is essential and a sweater should also be packed as the evenings can be quite chilly.

Ethiopians tend to be fairly formal and conservative in their dress — suits and ties being standard in Government and business offices.

It is necessary to remove one's shoes when entering churches and mosques and it is wise to bring along a pair of thick socks to wear as protection against splinters.